LOSING THE GOLDEN HOUR

ADST–DACOR Diplomats and Diplomacy Series

Since 1776, extraordinary men and women have represented the United States abroad under all sorts of circumstances. What they did and how and why they did it remain little known to their compatriots. In 1995 the Association for Diplomatic Studies and Training (ADST) and Diplomatic and Consular Officers, Retired, Inc. (DACOR) created the *Diplomats and Diplomacy* book series to increase public knowledge and appreciation of the involvement of American diplomats in world history. The series seeks to demystify diplomacy by telling the story of those who have conducted our foreign relations, as they lived, influenced, and reported them. *Losing the Golden Hour: An Insider's View of Iraq's Reconstruction* by James Stephenson is the thirty-first volume in the series.

Other Titles in the Series

Brown, Gordon, *Toussaint's Clause: The Founding Fathers and the Haitian Revolution*
Cohen, Herman J., *Intervening in Africa: Superpower Peacemaking in a Troubled Continent*
Cross, Charles T., *Born a Foreigner: A Memoir of the American Presence in Asia*
Grove, Brandon, *Behind Embassy Walls: The Life and Times of an American Diplomat*
Hart, Parker T., *Saudi Arabia and the United States: Birth of a Security Partnership*
Hume, Cameron R., *Mission to Algiers: Diplomacy by Engagement*
Kux, Dennis, *The United States and Pakistan, 1947–2000: Disenchanted Allies*
Loeffler, Jane C., *Architecture of Diplomacy: Building America's Embassies*
McNamara, Terry, *Escape with Honor: My Last Hours in Vietnam*
Miller, Robert H., *Vietnam and Beyond: A Diplomat's Cold War Education*
Parker, Richard B., *Uncle Sam in Barbary: A Diplomatic History*
Pezzullo, Ralph, *Plunging into Haiti: Clinton, Aristide, and the Defeat of Diplomacy*
Schaffer, Howard B., *Ellsworth Bunker: Global Troubleshooter, Vietnam Hawk*
Simpson, Howard R., *Bush Hat, Black Tie: Adventures of a Foreign Service Officer*

LOSING THE GOLDEN HOUR

*An Insider's View
of Iraq's Reconstruction*

JAMES STEPHENSON

FOREWORD BY RICHARD L. ARMITAGE

An ADST–DACOR Diplomats and Diplomacy Book

Potomac Books, Inc.
Washington, D.C.

Library of Congress Cataloging-in-Publication Data

Stephenson, James, 1946-
  Losing the golden hour : an insider's view of Iraq's reconstruction /
James Stephenson ; foreword by Richard L. Armitage. — 1st ed.
      p. cm. — (An ADST-DACOR diplomats and diplomacy book)
   Includes index.
   ISBN 978-1-59797-151-5 (alk. paper)
   1. Postwar reconstruction—Iraq. 2. Humanitarian assistance—Iraq. 3.
Iraq War, 2003—Peace. 4. Stephenson, James, 1946- 5. United States.
Agency for International Development—Officials and employees—
Anecdotes. I. Title.
   DS79.769.S74 2007
   956.7044'31—dc22
                                    2007025125

ISBN: 978-1-59797-151-5

(alk. paper)

Printed in the United States of America on acid-free paper that meets the
American National Standards Institute Z39-48 Standard.

Potomac Books, Inc.
22841 Quicksilver Drive
Dulles, Virginia 20166

First Edition

10 9 8 7 6 5 4 3 2 1

To my mother, who taught me to write.
Her failing sight will not permit her to read this.
My father will read it to her.

Better a thousand days of tyranny than one day of chaos.

Islamic proverb

CONTENTS

FOREWORD

Notwithstanding the unpopularity of the Iraq War, the American public has demonstrated enormous respect for the skill, courage, and endurance of our service men and women. Now, through the eyes of a major and seasoned participant, for the first time, we see that State Department and U.S. Agency for International Development (USAID) civilians performed with the same zeal, courage, and dedication: They served alongside our military, sharing the same trials and tribulations. There is no difference between them except that these stalwart civilians are unarmed.

James "Spike" Stephenson paints a vivid picture of the chaos, tension, disorganization, and danger of the attempt at reconstruction in Iraq. Spike is not a neophyte. He grew up leading men in combat as a young Army officer in Vietnam. In a twenty-five-year career in USAID he served in seven countries either at war or struggling with a fragile peace. He has heard the deadly hum of bullets in Vietnam, Serbia, and El Salvador.

Spike is not trying to settle scores, although he had significant doubts about the wisdom of invading Iraq—he is simply recounting the turmoil of daily life in Baghdad. I remember vividly his in-brief with me. To know him is to have a deep confidence in his integrity and dedication. This is what I immediately felt. For me, his account fills in the blanks between policy decisions in Washington and implementation, or lack thereof, in Iraq. Not everyone will be happy with this account—certainly not Paul Bremer, nor for that matter the Bush administration. Spike is neither an optimist nor a pessimist regarding Iraq. He is a man who deals with things as they are. His view has developed over time that Iraq will not survive as a single entity but that the decision to divide must be their idea, not ours.

This narrative is a vivid reminder of the limits of American power. The efforts of well-meaning and hardworking Americans are not a substitute for cogent analysis, reflection, and introspection. There is no shame in acknowledging that a strategy is not working. There is tremendous shame in continuing a flawed strategy—it defines insanity (i.e., trying the same thing over and over again expecting a different result).

Against the backdrop of the recent report of the Special Inspector General for Iraq's Reconstruction, this account will be recommended reading for future policy makers.

Please view this work with an eye to the thousands of our fellow citizens who labor in difficult conditions all around the globe. There is nobility in their effort. The policies an administration sets should be worthy of them.

Hon. RICHARD L. ARMITAGE
Former Deputy Secretary of State

PREFACE

This book chronicles the thirteen months I spent in Iraq as mission director for the United States Agency for International Development (USAID). But the prologue lies in my childhood and years of experience that led me to Baghdad. When I was ten, my father joined what would become USAID and moved the family to a remote dam site in central India. We lived in India for six of my most formative years. I attended college in the United States and then served four years as a U.S. Army officer. During a tour in Vietnam, I learned how to lead men under difficult and dangerous circumstances, and I swore I never wanted to do it again. Law school and private practice followed, but I was bored. Invited to join USAID, virtually by happenstance, I was immediately sent to Egypt in the heady days after Camp David. Following my stint in Egypt, I went to Barbados, Grenada, and the civil war–torn El Salvador, where I spent seven years. In 1997, I was sworn in as the USAID mission director to Lebanon, which was struggling to rebuild after sixteen years of civil war. Three years later, the fall of Slobodan Milosevic took me to Serbia and Montenegro.

The cadre that handles diplomacy and foreign assistance in war zones is a small one, its members known as specialists in that art. By 2003, I had served in seven countries either at war or struggling with a fragile peace. We suffered defeats in some, won victory in others. Twenty-five years had passed in the blink of an eye, and I had become recognized as a leader in stabilizing and reconstructing fragile or failed states. When I was asked to take over the USAID program in Iraq, it came as no surprise, but I neither sought nor wanted the position. I knew just how shallow the talent pool was, however, and as a Foreign Service officer I had sworn to serve anywhere. Confident in my own abilities, I was naively sure of America's ability to focus its best talents and win the peace, even in the face of daunting challenges. After all, collectively we and our allies knew how to re-build nations. We had done it all over the world, and I had been a part of that accomplishment.

This book is not a treatise on policy or a memoir of my daily life. Others have written and criticized the policy that took us to war and its implementation once in Iraq. While I do include some of that, I write from the viewpoint of the practitioner on the ground and not as an investigative journalist. Others, with the advantage of hind-sight, have written eloquently on both the military and civilian ef-forts there. In this book, I have endeavored to give the reader a sense of what I knew and how I reacted in real time. Accordingly, I tell the story chronologically for the most part to re-create the environment in which decisions were made and actions taken—or not. Undoubt-edly, some readers will have a different view of the events that I dis-cuss, but they did not stand in my shoes or view them through the same lens, tempered by a unique perspective and responsibility.

The Department of Defense (DOD) almost exclusively conducted the planning for what the military calls "Phase IV," or Iraq's post-conflict stabilization and reconstruction. For the first fifteen months—April 2003 to June 2004—DOD also controlled its imple-mentation, first through the auspices of the short-lived Office of Re-construction and Humanitarian Assistance (ORHA) and then through the Coalition Provisional Authority (CPA). Both organizations were essentially civilian, and though they availed themselves of some ex-perienced officers from the Department of State, USAID, and other agencies, they relied heavily on temporary employees recruited and hired by the Pentagon. Few of these employees had any overseas experience, much less experience in post-conflict stabilization and reconstruction. This disadvantage was compounded by events, as Iraq quickly disintegrated into a virulent insurgency. It was anything but "post-conflict."

Stabilization consists of reestablishing law and order, public services, and economic activity. Reconstruction involves rebuilding the instruments of governance and civil society and takes years. In Iraq, stabilization was never achieved, but we nonetheless embarked on reconstruction. Unfortunately, the CPA saw reconstruction primarily as an effort to rebuild the physical infrastructure of Iraq, as if bricks and mortar could heal a deeply divided country traumatized by decades of brutality and misrule. Too late, it turned over stabilization and reconstruction efforts to the Department of State's career practitioners. By then, the entire venture had become a complex counterinsurgency—the hardest conflict for any government and its allies to win.

The literature on Iraq tends to make villains of those in the Pentagon who planned and ran the Phase IV enterprise, to concentrate on the most bizarre and incompetent of those who served in the CPA, and to focus on the excesses of the Green Zone. I saw no villainy, only incompetence and hubris. The Green Zone, a necessary haven, was populated by the well-meaning but often culturally insensitive in the Coalition. It was separated, not divorced, from the rest of Baghdad, but it was not the "Little America" that some have described.

Iraq has been—in blood and wealth—America's costliest foreign venture since Vietnam. This book tells what it was like to live and work in Iraq as a part of that venture.

ACKNOWLEDGMENTS

Any book results from the effort, encouragement, advice, and criticism of dedicated supporters of the author. Without the efforts of my agent, Margery Thompson, and the editing of Don McKeon, this work might never have been published. My colleagues Chris Milligan, Fernando Cossich, Kirpatrick Day, and, especially, Teddy Bryan all contributed with their constructive critical comments and recall better than mine. I am particularly indebted to my employer, Charito Kruvant of Creative Associates International, who gave me the time to write. David Wall of International Resources Group led the U.S. economic growth effort in Iraq during my tenure, and I am indebted to him for permitting me to use his firsthand account of the challenges of implementing one of the most important efforts in the Iraq reconstruction program (see appendix).

GLOSSARY

Apache American attack helicopter

BCT Brigade Combat Team

BIAP Baghdad International Airport

Black Hawk American utility helicopter

Chinook Twin-rotor American cargo helicopter

CJTF-7 Coalition Joint Task Force-7, military arm of the Coalition

Coalition Allied military and civilians in Iraq

Cobra American attack helicopter

CPA Coalition Provisional Authority

CSH combat support hospital

DFAC dining facility

DOD Department of Defense

DS State Department Bureau of Diplomatic Security

FAR Federal Acquisition Regulations

FAV fully armored vehicle

1st Cav U.S. Army 1st Cavalry Division

IRMO Iraq Reconstruction Management Office

Katusha Russian or Chinese surface-to-surface rocket, usually 122 mm

LPA USAID Legislative and Public Affairs

Medevac unarmed medical evacuation helicopter

MNFI Multi-National Forces Iraq, succeeded CJTF-7

NGO nongovernmental organization

NSC National Security Council

OMB Office of Management and Budget

ORHA Office of Reconstruction and Humanitarian Assistance

OTI USAID Office of Transition Initiatives

PCO Project Contracting Office, succeeded PMO

PMO Project Management Office

PRB Program Review Board

PSD private security detail
RSO Regional Security Officer
State Department of State
Supplemental $18.4 billion FY 2004 Supplemental

appropriation for Iraq
SVTC secure video teleconference
USAID United States Agency for International Development

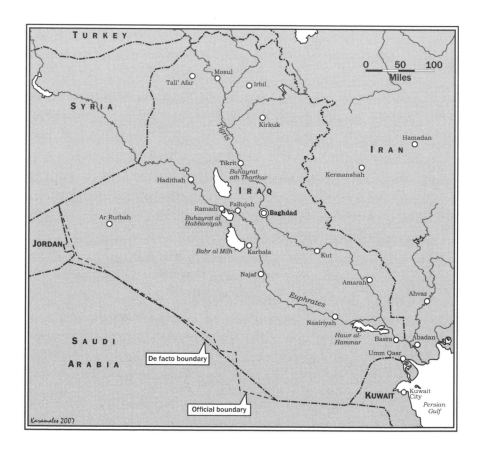

1

THE CALL

I was reclining in a dentist's chair and having my teeth cleaned, when my cell phone started to vibrate and then ring. Scrambling to rid myself of the suction tube in my mouth and sit up without smashing my head on the surgical light, I could read on the screen that it was an overseas call. Signaling my apologies to the dentist, I moved to the window, looked out over the rooftops at a gray evening, and answered the phone.

"Hello?"

"This is the State Department Operations Center trying to reach James Stephenson."

"This is he."

"Ambassador Chamberlin will speak to you."

It was Friday afternoon of Labor Day weekend 2003. I had been in Belgrade, the capital of Serbia and Montenegro, a remnant of the former Yugoslavia, for almost three years. As mission director for the United States Agency for International Development (USAID), I had built up a $150 million assistance program and led a staff of ninety people. I had been sent there two years earlier, when the program, and the Balkans, had been the hot item in the post-conflict transition business, because I was one of the top practitioners among a small cadre of Foreign Service officers who deal with the world's hot spots. The moment Slobodan Milosevic and the Balkans ceased to occupy center stage, I was at a conference in Sofia, Bulgaria. On the final day, as I was leaving the last meeting, a press attaché grabbed my arm and said, "Something terrible has happened." The date was September 11, 2001.

1

When the Taliban fell in late 2001, a colleague—another hot-zone practitioner—was pulled out of Kosovo to set up the Afghanistan USAID mission. Following his unplanned departure from Kabul in July 2003, the number two in my agency had pushed hard for me to immediately replace him, but I had too much on my plate. Plus I knew of the factors that had forced my friend to resign his post. I did not say "hell no," but I pushed back enough that I avoided an immediate transfer.

This phone call at the dentist's office was different. Ambassador Wendy Chamberlin was the assistant administrator of the Asia and Near East Bureau (ANE), and both Afghanistan and Iraq fell within her responsibility. As soon as I heard the operator mention her name, I knew what was coming.

"Is this Spike Stephenson?

"Yes, it is."

"Spike, this is Wendy Chamberlin. You do not know me, but I know of you and your reputation. I am going to ask you to do something very difficult, and I hope you will say yes."

"Go ahead."

"Spike, I want you to take over the mission in Iraq."

"Oh, boy. When would you want me?"

"May."

"Madam Ambassador, when do you need an answer?"

"Immediately."

"Well, let me have the weekend, and it will be waiting for you Tuesday morning."

"That will be fine."

Ringing off, I turned to my dentist and his assistant, who had heard my end of the conversation. "They want me to go to Baghdad."

"Oh, my God." He translated for the assistant, who immediately began to tear up.

"It's okay. Let's finish this, and let me get back to the office. It will be okay."

"My friend, must you go to that horrible place?"

"Yes, it's what I do—and I must."

During the buildup for Iraq, the overstretched USAID had reached back to a retired mission director, Lew Lucke, to lead the effort in Iraq. Lew was scheduled to leave Iraq in May 2004 for an ambassadorship. He and I were good friends.

With much on my mind, I left the dentist's office and returned to the embassy. Immediately I received a call from Gordon West, Ambassador Chamberlin's deputy. Gordon and I had known each other for years. I took the call in the courtyard, pacing back and forth on the sidewalk, smoking a cigar. Gordon apologized that he had been unable to give me any warning. I asked a few questions about the mission but told him there was no question about my decision. As a career officer, this request was not one to which I could say no, but I did want the weekend to break the news to my family.

While I was pacing and talking, my controller and my executive officer had come outside for a break. They were sitting on the wall as I paced. When I hung up, they both asked what was wrong. The three of us shared a small apartment building, and we were particularly close. I told them, "I just got the call I've been expecting. They want me to take Baghdad."

"Oh, no."

"Oh, yes."

"When?"

"May. It is not something to which I can say no."

It was a very long weekend, but on Tuesday morning I e-mailed Ambassador Chamberlin: "I'll do it." Little did I know that I would be doing it much sooner than May.

In late September, I returned to Washington for consultations and to attend a conference of mission directors. I had a chance to talk to Gordon West and Lew Lucke and to hear firsthand their assessment of how things were going in Iraq. At that time, Iraq was no more violent than other places where I had worked, such as Lebanon and El Salvador, and both men were upbeat. I returned directly to Montenegro, where we were holding an annual retreat for the entire mission. I broke the news to everyone on the retreat's last day. They were saddened but seemed unsurprised. Later, some would follow me to Iraq.

In late November, Gordon called. He and USAID administrator Andrew Natsios had just returned from Iraq. Since our last meeting, things had apparently changed a great deal.

"Spike, we want you to go now."

"Why? What's happened?"

"Look, Lew's been in theater since last February, and he's showing the strain. Andrew and I think we need a change, and we need to get you out there as soon as possible."

"Gordon, I have a huge meeting on Serbia in Washington in early January that my ambassador and I must do. I cannot possibly leave here before then."

"Andrew wants you out there, now, but I'll talk to him."

"Does Lew know about this?"

"Not yet. We wanted to talk to you first."

"Gordon, Lew and I are friends. I do not want to be the instrument of harm to him or his reputation."

"It's not like that. Lew will not be harmed. I'll try to hold Andrew off until the end of January, but I can't buy you any more time. Hopefully, Lew and you can pass through at the same time. Spike, I'm sorry about this, but there it is."

"I know."

Gordon was as good as his word and bought me the time I needed. Meanwhile, Ambassador L. Paul Bremer III, administrator of the Coalition Provisional Authority (CPA), had been forced to announce the CPA would hand over sovereignty to Iraq by June 30, 2004. I departed Belgrade for Washington on February 6. By that time, it was evident the USAID/Iraq mission's relationship with Bremer and the CPA was rocky, but it was also inevitable the CPA would hand over the reins to a new U.S. embassy on June 30.

In my predeparture meeting with Andrew Natsios, he made it clear that I had been chosen as the mission director because of my reputation for starting up big programs in tough places and for getting the job done while maintaining high staff morale. I had also been chosen because of my background as a U.S. Army officer and combat veteran, for we needed to develop closer relationships with the

Department of Defense (DOD). He outlined three objectives, in addition to running the mission:

- ✓ develop more programs that were transformational—that is, that would transform Iraq into a democracy with a free-market economy;
- ✓ be a good servant to the CPA and maintain a productive relationship with Ambassador Bremer and the military; and
- ✓ assist the State Department in the transition from the CPA to the embassy while protecting USAID's equities.

This meeting was followed by a round of meetings with the National Security Council (NSC), the Office of Management and Budget (OMB), the State Department, the Central Intelligence Agency (CIA), DOD, and various USAID offices supporting Iraq. One of my earliest appointments was with Robin Cleveland, a senior official at OMB. She had previously been a senior majority staffer at the Senate Appropriations Committee's Subcommittee for Foreign Operations, and I knew her well. Robin had pushed hard for my assignment to Serbia and Montenegro and was supportive of the assignment to Iraq.

Congress had recently approved the $18.4 billion supplemental appropriation for Iraq, and an intense and continuing turf battle ensued over the program's content and who would take the lead on its implementation. USAID and State had been closed out of the CPA's development of the program, and when it was presented to Congress, they were stunned to learn it consisted almost entirely of large infrastructure projects across ten sectors. Supported by others, their protests had resulted in the "reservation" of $4 billion of the total whose use was to be deferred until State succeeded the CPA. The CPA, which answered to DOD, had created an ad hoc entity, the Program Management Office (PMO), to manage the design and implementation of the thousands of projects that made up the $18.4 billion. The PMO never allocated the $4 billion reserve against an equivalent amount in projects, however, and considered them still on the table.

Robin was well known for her direct manner, intolerance for prevarication and obfuscation, and brutal candor. I always enjoyed meeting with her, but many of my colleagues dreaded the prospect. I was barely seated before she asked why the CPA had created the PMO since its mission seemed identical to that normally performed by USAID. Was it not superfluous? Couldn't the mission and I manage the entire $18.4 billion program? I answered that taking over the entire Iraq program was not in my brief, nor was it realistic. USAID's largest country program to date had been in Egypt, which had peaked at about $1 billion per year. My brief from Andrew Natsios was to work with the CPA, not to draw USAID further into a turf battle. I agreed with Robin that the PMO's stated mission sounded very much like USAID's normal mission but also noted a program of this size had not been attempted since the Marshall Plan. I would have my hands full with the current $2 billion program, and it was slated to grow. Besides, I pointed out, we simply did not have the capacity to run an $18.4 billion program alone. Another relevant truth was I did not want to poison my relationship with Ambassador Bremer and DOD before I even arrived.

While Robin was not entirely happy with my answers, I believe she recognized the die was already cast. As a consolation, she arranged meetings for me with Deputy Secretary of Defense Paul Wolfowitz and Deputy Secretary of State Richard Armitage.

In spite of my professional willingness to go to Iraq, I had not supported the decision to invade Iraq. My opposition was not on moral grounds or any concern about whether Saddam Hussein did or did not have weapons of mass destruction (WMD). After eight years' experience in the Middle East, I feared such an incursion would leave the United States open to becoming the target of every competing faction in Iraq and of its neighbors that wanted us to fail. Everything I had read and heard since the invasion validated my fears that we were being drawn deeper into counterinsurgency operations that would leave us mired in Iraq for years. Having been intimately involved in counterinsurgencies in Vietnam and El Salvador, I agreed with T. E. Lawrence that counterinsurgency is "messy and slow . . . like eating soup with a knife." As it was, however, the Bush administration was not even admitting we were engaged in counterinsurgency, prefer- ring to label the Sunni insurgents "dead-enders."

At that time, Paul Wolfowitz was reputed to be the neoconservative author of the war, and I was curious to meet him. I was surprised at his gentility, candor, and keen interest. He listened a great deal more than he talked in that first meeting. Later I came to believe he had been seduced by the siren songs of Iraqi exiles and had ignored or discounted the advice and intelligence of seasoned career analysts at the Defense Intelligence Agency (DIA). He paid far more attention to the advice of Iraq exiles and bloggers than sea- soned professionals in the Pentagon and other agencies.

Richard Armitage was legendary. A decorated U.S. Naval of- ficer who served three combat tours in Vietnam, longtime policy maker, and burly bodybuilder, he was not the kind of person usually found on the seventh floor of the State Department—not even in Colin Powell's State Department. At the higher levels of State, one guest rarely meets alone with anyone; rather, the convention is that peers, note takers, principals, and guests sit in a conversational group. Armitage barreled into the room like a squat locomotive, donned a windbreaker (it was always cold on the seventh floor), offered cof- fee, had me sit across his desk from him, and launched into a ma- chine-gun staccato of questions. The others sat across the room on the couches and chairs. Armitage is personable, no-nonsense, and entirely likable. I took away from our conversation that he was not a fan of L. Paul Bremer and feared that State, having been largely ex- cluded from the planning of the Iraq reconstruction program, was now going to be left holding the bag. He carefully took my measure and asked me to work with the State and DOD team to make the transition as smooth as possible. Along with Colin Powell, Armitage would resign in less than a year, but during his tenure, he was always supportive of me personally and of the USAID mission in Iraq.

The meetings with the NSC members were bizarre, even though at least one was with a USAID colleague seconded to the NSC. Al- though the NSC would later attempt to micromanage much of the reconstruction program, the only substantive meeting I had was with former ambassador Shirin Tahir-Kheli, whose sole interest was the

Basra Children's Hospital. She let it be known that this project was of the utmost priority to First Lady Laura Bush and the administration and inferred that my success or failure depended on getting it built. Apparently Tahir-Kheli herself had promised Basra officials a $500 million teaching hospital, which Congress had promptly zeroed out of the supplemental appropriation. Congress later relented but capped the hospital's construction at $50 million, and even that figure was a grudging concession. The Basra hospital project would prove to be a sideshow that would occupy enormous time and energy and for little gain. (The Basra Hospital would gain notoriety in 2006 when USAID, in a rancorous exchange of letters with the special inspector general for Iraq, was accused of deliberately concealing indirect costs associated with the overall cost of its construction.) I made a point of avoiding meeting with her again and succeeded.

Ambassador Frank Ricciardone and Lt. Gen. (Ret.) Claude "Mick" Kicklighter, USA, had been tapped to lead the Iraq program's transition from DOD to State control. Both proved to be able, reasonable, and approachable. At our initial meeting, the first words out of Frank Ricciardone's mouth were, "I have just returned from Baghdad, and the CPA is the most dysfunctional organization I have ever seen. I've never seen so many well-meaning people doing the wrong thing." Though his assessment was sobering, I liked him immediately, and we would develop a strong relationship in the battles to come. General Kicklighter was in a difficult position. He owed allegiance to the secretary of defense, but he was a straight shooter who called them as he saw them. I liked and respected him as well.

My most curious meeting was with Rear Adm. (Ret.) David Nash in the Pentagon. A CPA adviser to the Iraq Ministry of Transportation, Nash had been tapped by Ambassador Bremer to develop what became the $18.4 billion program. Nash believed the program needed to be managed by a single agency and had convinced Bremer and DOD to create the Program Management Office. The PMO ran the entire program, and Nash ran the PMO. No implementing entity, including USAID, would receive funds except through the PMO, and the PMO would be the largest implementing entity. Nash was already miffed at USAID over the $4 billion reservation from the $18.4

billion and what he perceived as the delay USAID and State had thereby caused the PMO in contracting for program management and construction. He looked the part of a retired admiral—lean, alert, gray-haired, confident, and wary. At our first meeting, I tried to reassure him my brief was to work as part of a team, there was plenty of work for all of us, and I was an experienced practitioner of reconstruction and stabilization programs in challenging environments. His wariness belied his affability, and I departed with all of my internal alarms sounding.

Some of my last meetings were with Ambassador John D. Negroponte and Ambassador James Jeffrey. Negroponte had just been named U.S. ambassador to Iraq, and Jeffrey would be the deputy chief of mission (DCM) at the U.S. embassy in Iraq. Both came across as experienced, smart, and no one's fools, and I liked both men. It was a strong team, but none of us could have known what was waiting for us in Iraq.

As the days dwindled down, I finished the rounds of consultations, spent time visiting my far-flung family, stayed a few nights with my aging parents, and wrote a new will. Leaving Dulles Airport was all too familiar—as if I were stepping off, in the dark, into thin air. After tours in five hot zones, I knew what I was doing, but I still felt the grip in the pit of my stomach. My loved ones were supportive but almost catatonic with fear for my safety.

2 SPIRALING INTO GÖTTERDÄMMERUNG

Most official travel from the United States to Iraq involved a flight to Europe, a connection to Kuwait, and a wait for a C-130 military transport to Baghdad International Airport, now infamously known as BIAP. In addition to the civilian airport, BIAP contained a military airport and a vast collection of U.S. military facilities. Early on, USAID had contracted Air Serv International, a charter service that operates in challenging environments. Air Serv flew twin-engine commuter aircraft out of Amman, Jordan, to Baghdad, Basra, and Irbil. The arrangement with Air Serv proved to be a godsend that enabled our staff, as well as thousands of employees of nongovernmental organizations (NGOs), to get in and out of Iraq without having to resort to military transport or endure days-long waits at BIAP. Air Serv employed mostly laconic South African pilots, who were experienced at evasive action and utterly unflappable.

A day of meetings at the U.S. embassy and USAID mission in Amman gave me the opportunity to deal with issues related to billeting there some families of our Iraq-based Foreign Service officers and to setting up some of our accounting, contracting, and service operations in the embassy. The latter efforts were successful, but the State Department steadfastly opposed any move to place Foreign Service families in Amman, where they would be closer to loved ones serving in Iraq. No doubt, the department had valid administrative, diplomatic, and security concerns that influenced the decision, but it would cause the Iraq mission significant problems in recruiting and retaining staff.

11

The day of meetings also allowed me to rest up in a four-star hotel, the staff of which would come to know me well over the next year. Amman was still sleeping on February 20, 2004, when I took a taxi to Marka Airport and boarded Air Serv for the two-hour flight to Baghdad. As the plane climbed to altitude, I could see the snow-covered mountains of Lebanon, where I had lived and worked for three years. The sight of them gave me a lift and seemed a good omen.

BIAP covers an immense area. It is not large enough, however, to prevent insurgents from getting close and firing man-portable air defense systems (MANPADS), shoulder-launched heat-seeking missiles, at landing and departing aircraft with alarming frequency. To make for a more difficult target, pilots avoid long final approaches or climb-outs and spiral in or out, right over the airport. The Air Serv drill was to circle the airport at 22,000 feet, throw the wing over into a tight spiral, descend at a stomach-churning 65-degree angle, and level out just above the runway. Takeoff was the exact reverse. I rather enjoyed the ride, as did the pilots. Though my flights were never shot at by a MANPADS during my tenure, I still habitually sat at the rear of the cabin and as far away as possible from the heat signature of the engine exhausts.

The civilian side of BIAP was an international airport in name only. Although USAID was successfully completing a number of projects to restore the facilities and train personnel to international standards, commercial passenger service was scant. Only one concourse was being used and just barely. Our plane parked on the tarmac, and the passengers marched through a glass door to Immigration. Processing, retrieving our luggage, and passing through a dimly lit Customs area took about five minutes. No one stamped our passports; instead, the important document here was the DOD identification called a "Common Access Card" (CAC). Outside in bright sunlight was a small army of bodyguards, known as personal security details (PSDs), waiting for their passengers. Kroll, a private security firm, provided ours. My outgoing deputy and his replacement, Chris Milligan, were waiting for me with our PSD and two fully armored vehicles (FAVs). We introduced ourselves, shook hands, and departed. Offered an armored vest and Kevlar helmet, I declined, noticing that no one else was wearing them. It was the last time I would ride anywhere in the "Red Zone"—that is, anywhere outside the "Green Zone"—without the protection of full body armor.

The Green Zone is carved out of the center of Baghdad. Situated on a bend of the Tigris River, it is about five square miles and surrounded by a wall of eighteen-foot-high, prefabricated, concrete "T-barriers." The wall intersects major thoroughfares, and within its confines are the former ministries and palaces of Saddam, his relatives, and demented offspring. Precision-guided weapons targeted most of these sites the first night of the war, and their bombed skeletons litter the Green Zone. The CPA's headquarters was the Republican Palace, which predated Saddam as the seat of Iraq's national government. It had been spared in the bombing.

The road from Baghdad International Airport to the Green Zone runs east and is best negotiated at high speed. The journey is only six or seven miles and takes either ten minutes or the rest of your life. Although it was already reputed to be the most dangerous road in the world, it would become more deadly once improvised explosive devices (IEDs) and suicide bombers became the insurgents' weapons of choice. Still, our PSD's shoulders visibly lifted when we rolled through the Green Zone's military checkpoint at Gate 12.

By the time I arrived, Hussein's adornments—giant metal reproductions of his helmeted head—had been removed from the palace. An enormous, two-story building with a stone façade, it housed offices, a dining facility (DFAC), a chapel, and a dormitory for those waiting to be assigned a trailer. The palace had been surrounded on three sides by ancient groves of date palms, but these had been cut down to accommodate the sea of trailers and tents that housed most of the CPA.

At that time, the Green Zone had not been carved up into T-barrier-enclosed compounds, as it would be later, and there were few checkpoints within the zone itself. Thousands of Iraqis lived in bungalows and apartment buildings inside the zone. Located at the zone's northwest edge, the USAID mission was on the third floor of the Convention Center and across the street from the Al Rashid Hotel, which had been largely empty following a rocket attack in October

2003. We also maintained a small liaison office in the Republican Palace to interact with the CPA and the military.

My predecessor had persuaded the CPA to permit USAID to build a residential sixteen-acre compound on the Green Zone's northeast edge in an area that bordered the Tigris. When I arrived, three small masonry houses had been completed, and crews were just breaking ground on eighty more. Most of our expatriate staffers were housed in trailers on the compound, but many were living in bungalows, or the "villas," scattered around the Green Zone. The compound was not yet enclosed, and it was filled with Iraqi construction workers throughout the day. Our guard force consisted simply of two Gurkhas standing at a drop bar. Staff sometimes had sundown picnics on the exposed bank of the river. We ate in various military dining facilities managed by Kellogg, Brown and Root (KBR), which also provided laundry and other services. Throughout the zone were small restaurants, such as the Green Zone Café, and even smaller Iraqi-operated mom-and-pop stores.

In those first days, I could not help but be reminded of Vietnam, where I had served thirty-three years earlier. Soldiers, Humvees, Abrams tanks, and Bradley fighting vehicles were everywhere. The drone of helicopters landing and departing from Landing Zone (LZ) Washington (the Green Zone helipad) and of medevacs landing at the combat support hospital (CHS, pronounced "Cash") was constant. All the expatriates except us appeared to be armed. As a policy, our staff and contractors were not permitted to carry weapons, though the Kroll PSDs accompanied and protected us whenever we left the Green Zone. Nevertheless, the Green Zone, my home for the next thirteen months, was a relatively benign and seemingly safe environment—a world away from what was going on outside its concrete walls.

All in all, those first days and weeks gave me the impression my tour was going to be a walk in the park—that Iraq, as El Salvador and Lebanon had proved, was not nearly as difficult or dangerous as billed by the press. Even a trip up-country in early March, by plane, helicopter, and vehicle, to Mosul, Irbil, and Kirkuk did not dissuade me from that impression. This tour was going to be great. Hell, I thought, I might even stay for two years.

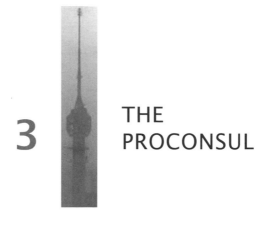

3　THE PROCONSUL

While still in Washington, it had been made clear to me that USAID was not in good standing with Ambassador L. Paul Bremer, or Jerry, as his friends called him. On several occasions, he had reportedly even threatened to kick the agency out of Iraq. It was notable that the CPA's website, which touted a number of accomplishments in reconstruction, did not mention that most were USAID's projects. Having repeatedly heard and sensed the enmity, I asked Lew Lucke why it was so. Lew discounted it, saying that at his farewell Bremer had lauded his and USAID's efforts. He felt perhaps we just needed to do a better job of making the CPA appreciate our value.

Upon my arrival, I immediately saw that the source of the enmity probably had more to do with USAID's historical independence and Bremer's perceiving it as a somewhat loose cog in the CPA machine, which he viewed as *his* machine. USAID is an independent U.S. government agency created by the Foreign Assistance Act of 1961. While the agency receives policy guidance from the Department of State, it does have a voice in the development of policy. Overseas, USAID is often the largest entity within a U.S. embassy and normally enjoys significant independence in designing and implementing foreign assistance programs. To Bremer, USAID was a tool— an executing agency—whose members were rarely privy to policy making or even to determining their own programs' direction. Not surprisingly then, during the CPA's four remaining months, my relationship with Ambassador Bremer was cordial but never close, and often on the verge of rupture.

The CPA was a bloated organization that combined the structures of a shadow government and the administrative divisions necessary to support it. Most CPA employees were "3161" temporary employees, so called after the DOD temporary authority under which they were hired. Many of them spent only three to six months in Iraq and were on their first trip overseas. Few had any overseas development experience, and many were former Republican Party campaign workers, supporters, and fund-raisers or Bush administration political appointees. There were also some talented Foreign Service officers, seconded to the CPA by the State Department; a large contingent of seconded and retired military officers provided by DOD; and even individuals hired by USAID and seconded directly to the CPA. We called the latter "Free Ions," because we had no control over them and often found them working against our interests. (I sent home all the Free Ions after the CPA's demise.) Finally, the Coalition included a modest contingent of non-U.S. civilian and military members, with the British having the greatest number.

The Republican Palace was a vast building, filled to the rafters with people who were busy from early morning until late at night. Whole sections were occupied by "ministries," or the shadow ministries of CPA employees who occupied and ran Iraq. In addition to the offices in the palace, each ministry had offices in the real Iraqi ministries, where CPA staff ventured out to work with the respective ministry and its staff. The CPA shadow ministers were called "senior advisers." A few had specific subject and area skills, and they did well, in spite of an almost total lack of overseas experience and no post-conflict development experience. But most advisers were learning on the job, with an astounding lack of preparation in either life experiences or training. More than a small number could only be described as "loons," who pursued pet agendas, oblivious to the damage they could cause. Unfortunately, all were generously empowered to run Iraq on behalf of Ambassador Bremer and the CPA. It was their "most excellent adventure," and we were along for the ride.

Outside the Green Zone, the CPA maintained regional coordinators who covered all the provinces of Iraq. Many of them were experienced U.S. and British Foreign Service officers.

They interacted with local military commanders, Iraqi provincial officials, local sheikhs, and average Iraqis. Some behaved like minor viceroys, but most comported themselves with competence and little guidance from the Green Zone. All took enormous risks to their personal safety. Periodically, they came in for a commanders' and coordinators' conference with Bremer and Lt. Gen. Ricardo Sanchez, the Coalition Joint Task Force 7 commander. It provided an opportunity for the CPA and military leadership to hear the truth from people in the field about the performance of the Coalition's program.

As director of the USAID mission, I was, lamentably, more an observer than a participant in these meetings. In fact, my staff had to battle to have me invited at all, and the CPA made it clear that my place was not at the table but along the wall. Bremer ran the conference and used it as a forum to impart information and give direction. The one time I heard a dedicated and competent regional coordinator express cogent dissent against the CPA program, Bremer curtly dismissed it, demonstrating to the dissenter and everyone else in the room that dissent was not welcome.

My routine contact with Ambassador Bremer was at the daily senior staff meeting, which was held every morning but Friday at eight o'clock. (On Fridays, in deference to Bremer's encouragement that we not work that morning, senior staff met at noon.) The meetings were held in a large reception room that had been converted into a conference room after placing tables together to make one large conference table, perhaps forty feet long by twelve feet wide. Around the table were about forty black faux-leather swivel chairs, half of which were broken. Behind these, straight-backed and folding chairs for aides, deputies, and late arrivals lined the walls. An overflow crowd always stood clustered around the doorway. Regulars gathered a few minutes before eight, jealously guarding their places at the table. Four seats, facing the door, were reserved for Bremer and his deputies, who attended an earlier scheduled meeting.

Bremer was punctual, and the room was usually full when he swept through the door. He invariably wore a green quilted hiking vest, a French-cuffed dress shirt, and a tie. He is an imposing man with chiseled good looks and very good hair. He has a ready smile and wry sense of humor that offsets his impatience and generally masks his temper. He is self-assured and comes across as both personable and arrogant. As he took his seat at meetings, he usually looked directly at several of the staff or guests and acknowledged them by name and with a warm nod. He began with either a direct query to a participant or announced that he had nothing to say. He then turned to his left, and the opportunity to speak moved clockwise around the table and then counterclockwise through the outer circle. Bremer ran the meeting. Rarely did anyone else—not generals, not ambassadors—speak. The meeting was normally over by 8:10. Most of the senior staff then headed for breakfast at the palace's dining facility, which closed at 8:30.

I also had a weekly private meeting with Ambassador Bremer. To access his office, one entered from the gallery beneath the palace's imposing blue central dome. The desks of perhaps a dozen aides flanked what had been a large reception area opening to a courtyard. To the left were the aides and office of Sir Jeremy Greenstock, the political leader of the British contingent. To the right, one passed through a corridor where Americans manned desks and approached a large wooden door guarded by a secretary and a bodyguard provided by Blackwater, the private security company that guarded Ambassador Bremer everywhere he went. There visitors stood until admitted by the secretary.

I generally took my deputy, Chris Milligan, and sometimes other staff members to these meetings. Chris had been one of the first civilians in Iraq after the Iraqi Army fell and had managed our palace liaison office. He had dealt closely with Bremer for nine months and knew what would tweak his enthusiasm and what would send him up the wall. Our routine was to manage the agenda and save any contentious issues for the third quarter of the meeting and give him a fourth-quarter finish that would leave him happy. When this approach was not possible, it made for a very long half hour.

The meetings usually began with Bremer coming from behind his desk, warmly welcoming us and bidding us to sit around a coffee table, upon which he usually placed his desert combat boots. We would hand him the agenda—usually spiced with progress on activities he liked—and then I would work briskly through it. Chris would weigh in where needed. Bremer was always interested and asked cogent questions. He would often exclaim, "This is great!" But if he did not like something, his mood would change instantly, sometimes followed by affirmations that *he* was in charge, that *he* talked to the president, that *he* made policy.

It was not the first time I had worked for an ambassador with a reputation for knowing what he wanted, for bludgeoning anyone he perceived to stand in his way. USAID mission directors and CIA station chiefs generally have more independence and latitude to stand up to an ambassador than does anyone else in an embassy. In high-profile countries, where much is at stake, the business of advice and consent can get contentious, but I had always managed to develop close and mutually supportive partnerships with my ambassadors, even when disagreeing with them or giving them advice they did not want to hear. However, it became evident early on that Ambassador Bremer was not receptive to advice and was actively hostile to any that went against his own judgment. Perhaps he took it from others, but he rarely did from me. That was his prerogative, but it was not good leadership.

In fairness, many CPA personnel remain intensely loyal to Jerry Bremer and probably outnumber those of his critics who served in Iraq. I well remember the tearful farewell speeches of departing senior staff members who lauded him for what they genuinely considered his enlightened leadership and perspicacity. After the CPA's demise and amid its wreckage, many of those who stayed on would long for its halcyon days.

Ambassador Bremer's signature item from his wardrobe was those buff military desert boots, which he wore even with dress suits and after he left Iraq. They were undoubtedly comfortable and did not show the dust that immediately coated polished shoes. Although virtually no one but Bremer wore suits, one could not help but notice the coterie around him—all outfitted with buff military boots. Early in my tour, I acquired a pair of military desert boots and wore them once to our weekly USAID staff meeting, where I was assailed with jests that I had been "Bremerized" and gone over to the "dark side." They did not fit, but that was not the reason I never wore them again.

I will always be conflicted about Bremer. He was smart, worked grueling hours, and took on the toughest job of any American envoy since Vietnam. He had made his bones in the State Department by serving a number of secretaries of state as an executive secretary. Prior to Iraq, he had been the ambassador to the Netherlands and the ambassador-at-large for counterterrorism. After his retirement, he had an executive position in Henry Kissinger's consulting firm and, later, served as the chief executive officer of Marsh Crisis Consulting. Although his credentials were impressive, his experience did not prepare him for the challenges of transforming a traumatized, deeply divided society into a viable democracy with a free-market economy and with the ability to protect itself from hostile neighbors.

I do not fault Bremer alone for the spectacular mistakes made by the CPA, DOD, and White House: the disbanding of the Iraqi Army, the de-Baathification policy, and the delay in creating an Iraqi government. Many must share the responsibility for those decisions. He was not even responsible for the generally poor quality of the personnel whom DOD hired for the CPA. I do fault him, however, for accepting their counsel, for the arrogance and hubris that seemingly emboldened him to continue on a course that was so obviously misguided, and for ignoring fifty years of U.S. experience in post-conflict nation building.

I fault myself as well for not directly confronting Bremer with my concerns that the reconstruction program was poorly conceived and would fail. Frankly, I thought doing so would win me nothing but a one-way trip home and leave my staff unprotected. I thought we could outlast Bremer and the CPA and, under new management, modify the reconstruction program. I still do not believe a confrontation would have accomplished anything positive, but I did not try and therefore will never know. For me, Bremer remains an enigma.

4 INTERREGNUM

What was the American experience in post-conflict nation building that I felt Ambassador Bremer was squandering? My observations and thoughts then were grounded in my twenty-five years' experience as a practitioner of stabilization and reconstruction in countries mired in conflict or emerging from it. Through trial, error, failure, and success, all practitioners—Western governments, the United Nations, the World Bank, bilateral aid agencies, nongovernmental organizations, and contractors—had learned there are three critical elements of stabilization and reconstruction: security, democracy, and economic growth. All are relative terms, depending on conditions in a particular country, and all are moving targets that are changing and require constant adjustment.

Establishing security involves domestic security, secure borders, and relatively accommodating neighbors. Of the three factors in achieving stabilization and reconstruction, domestic security is the most important and often the most difficult to achieve. Breakdowns in domestic security may be caused by insurgency, organized crime, or internal security forces that are abusive, corrupt, ineffective, or a combination of all three. In El Salvador, for example, the three national police forces could maintain order, but they were highly abusive, corrupt, and responsible for extrajudicial killings of dissidents and innocents. A key demand of the Frente Faribundo Marti para Liberación Nacional (FMLN)—an umbrella of the five guerrilla groups that fought against the government of El Salvador— was that the government had to disband the national police forces.

The peace agreement signed in 1992 mandated a new force under civilian control.

Unfortunately, effective police forces require extensive training, and events conspired to open a "security gap." With peace, thousands of soldiers from both sides were demobilized. Though efforts were made to integrate former soldiers into society, some chose to continue to use their acquired martial skills in the pursuit of crime. At the same time, the U.S. penal system, which had incarcerated thousands of Salvadoran gang members for crimes committed in the United States, began to deport those who were illegal aliens to El Salvador. They exited the plane in El Salvador as free men and immediately began establishing the same gangs. The nascent national police force was overwhelmed. Though the civil war had ended, the country was plunged into the new terror of murder, kidnapping, and armed robbery for profit. This security gap threatened the otherwise successful democratic and economic transition that was taking place.

The military component of the U.S. counterinsurgency effort in El Salvador consisted of training forces, supplying equipment, and sharing intelligence. Still stinging from the defeat in Vietnam, Congress had capped the number of military advisers who could serve in El Salvador and prohibited direct combat support, including air support. Thus it took years to raise the capabilities of the Salvadoran military, which was never able to completely defeat the FMLN. While the military was being supported, the State Department and USAID concentrated on democratization and economic growth. They largely accomplished this effort through creating and backing indigenous NGOs committed to democratic governance and a free-market economy. It took years to develop democratic institutions and emplace policies conducive to civil order and growth. However, these were only the building blocks.

To end a civil war, all the parties have to want it to end, or one group must defeat all others. In November 1989, the FMLN launched the bloodiest offensive of the war against the strength of the government, namely, the cities. To that point, the war had been a stalemate, with the FMLN in relative control of large parts of the north and east of the country and with the government in control of the cities and most productive agricultural areas. But the tide was running against the FMLN. It could no longer count on materiel support from the crumbling Soviet Union and its client Cuba. Liberation theology and Marxism—the FMLN's political underpinning—were being repudiated throughout Latin America. The FMLN had not lost the war, but it could not win. Its November offensive was one last throw of the dice or a calculated gamble to increase the FMLN's bargaining position in eventual peace negotiations. The offensive caused almost three thousand deaths and almost $400 million in damages to vital infrastructure. It paralyzed the country for a month. When it ended, the FMLN had gained no territory, won no converts, and suffered heavy casualties. However, the offensive did terrify the ruling elites and convinced them that the war both had to end and could not be ended militarily. Both sides had been bled white.

Fortunately, most of the spadework of democratization and economic reform had already been accomplished. El Salvador had a freely elected right-of-center government with a dynamic leader, President Felix Cristiani. Much of the social justice the FMLN claimed to be fighting for had already been achieved. The FMLN began to put out feelers for a negotiated end to the civil war. Remarkably, the catalyst was a Democratic Senate staffer named Dick McCall, who was able to engage with the FMLN, the ruling elites, and President Cristiani. McCall convinced the FMLN leadership to invite U.S. ambassador William Walker and his key staff members to a parley at Santa Marta, a village in the heart of FMLN territory. Cristiani supported the meeting. It was a bold move and not without risk for the ambassador and his team.

The Santa Marta meeting opened a dialogue and, ironically, established the principle that the United States would ensure fair treatment of the FMLN during negotiations and in the eventual peace settlement. Immediate assistance from USAID to Santa Marta convinced the FMLN leadership the United States and Cristiani were serious about peace. Formal negotiations between the warring parties were held in Mexico City, but we all worked in the background. When the agreement was signed in 1992, it ratified the Salvadoran government's authority, the FMLN's legitimacy as a peaceful political opposition, the reduction of the Salvadoran military, the re-structuring of the national police, and the disarming and demobiliza-tion of the FMLN. It also mandated measures to reintegrate fighters from both sides into society. In the 1994 national elections, the parties of the former FMLN won sufficient seats in the National Assembly to become a strong, loyal opposition. It also supported the free-market economic reforms that were already propelling strong economic growth.

El Salvador was one case where the security gap did not de-rail the post-conflict transition, though it undoubtedly impeded economic growth. Good governance and the development of civil society prevailed.

In 1997 I went to Lebanon. Its civil war had ended in 1989 with the Taif Accords. By then, all sides had been bled out by fifteen years of fighting, but the best that the warring factions could obtain had been a return to the status quo ante. They maintained the constitu-tion, which mandated the apportionment of representation "by con-fession"—that is, by religion—and stipulated the president would be a Christian, the prime minister a Sunni Muslim, and the speaker of parliament a Shiite Muslim. Meanwhile, Syrian forces remained in Lebanon, and Israeli Defense Forces occupied southern Lebanon.

There was no catharsis. Everyone simply exhaled and resolved to get back to business. There was no census to determine what the real representation by confession should be, because that move threat-ened to upset the status quo. More important, no one addressed the causes of the civil war. Indeed, many Lebanese steadfastly maintained there had been *no* civil war and that the orgy of killing was the result of foreign agitation. All militias were supposed to disarm, but Hezbollah, the powerful Shiite militia supported by Iran and Syria, refused as long as Israel occupied Lebanese soil. Hezbollah success-fully billed itself as the "resistance," and the Lebanese government looked the other way because it was powerless to do anything about it. The government turned to the economic rebuilding of the country but made little effort at democratic reforms. It ignored Hezbollah's creation of a state within the state. When Israel ended its occupation of Lebanon in 2000, Hezbollah, to justify its arms, created the fiction that the Shebaa farms in the Golan Heights were Lebanese territory, even though the UN had certified that Israel had withdrawn from all Lebanese territory. In 2006, Hezbollah provoked a month-long war with Israel that killed hundreds of innocent Lebanese and devastated Lebanon's infrastructure. Today, Lebanon is once again in political turmoil, and many believe it is on the edge of renewed civil war.

Lebanon presents a case where, for understandable reasons, political leaders chose domestic security over democratic transformation. The factions agreed to stop fighting and permitted the Syrian occupation to ensure domestic security. It was not perfect security, but it was sufficient to allow everyone to get back to business. The physical rebuilding of Lebanon created the illusion of economic growth, while incurring massive debt, but domestic security allowed commerce to thrive and fortunes to be made. Unfortunately, it was a house of cards and will so remain until its leaders address fundamental issues of representation and the only armed forces in the country are the Lebanese Army and the police—not Hezbollah.

In February 2001, I arrived in the Federal Republic of Yugoslavia (FRY) to lead the USAID mission there. Following the Balkan wars of the 1990s, the Dayton Accords, and the 1999 NATO bombing of the FRY to end ethnic cleansing in Kosovo, the FRY had been reduced to the federal states of Serbia and Montenegro. Kosovo was technically still a part of the FRY but under UN administration and North Atlantic Treaty Organization (NATO) protection. In Serbia, elections and the 2000 October Revolution had swept into power a reform government led by Zoran Djindjic. His cabinet was populated with Western-educated technocrats who vowed to turn the FRY into a Western democracy with a free-market economy. They were young and dynamic, and we called them the "Dream Team."

After the fall of the Soviet Union, the United States and the European Union (EU) had lavished economic assistance on the former Eastern Bloc states with considerable success. Bulgaria, the Czech Republic, Estonia, Hungary, Latvia, Lithuania, Poland, Romania, Slovakia, and Slovenia—all had democratically elected governments that had converted from command economies to more free-market economies. All were on the path to joining the European Union. This transformation had been accomplished with the formula of security, democracy, and economic reform. Although in most cases the physical infrastructure—roads, transportation, power, and industry—was decayed, USAID did not engage heavily in rebuilding it. Instead, focusing on democratic governance and economic reform created the enabling environment that attracted public and private investment to the rebuilding. Reconstruction was not lightning fast, but its trajectory was constant. We had also learned that such a transition was painful and that the rising tide did not lift all boats at the same time. The states required more assistance to address the needs of those populations that were the last to benefit from reforms.

In the FRY, by contrast, we embarked on a program of rapid economic reform supported by a more modest program of democratic reform and a massive effort in community revitalization and local governance. The Djindjic government had been elected after promising rapid reforms of Serbia's stagnant economy and greater democratic freedom. Although Djindjic had the support of a majority of the electorate, elements in Serbia still preferred his predecessor, Slobodan Milosevic, and took a wait-and-see posture. The imperative of rapid economic reform was to realize tangible economic growth before the window of broad political support began to close.

The insistence of the United States and the Europeans that Serbian war criminals—beginning with Milosevic—be arrested and tried at the UN International War Crimes Tribunal at the Hague did not help the political situation. Serbs are proud of their heritage and resentful of the opprobrium attached to all of them for atrocities committed in the Balkan wars. The U.S. and European pressure angered Djindjic's opposition and even some of his supporters. What we did not know was that Djindjic's victory had stemmed from a deal cut with the Serbian paramilitary units and security forces. They would abandon Milosevic, but Djindjic had to leave them intact and untouched.

Initially, there was rapid progress in economic reform. But by mid-2002, the Dream Team was clearly slowing down. All our polling indicated the general public strongly supported even more rapid reform, but the government seemed distracted by political pressure and the burdens of simply governing. When the pace of reform started to wane, we commiserated. Instead, we should have given them tough love and assistance conditioned upon continued progress.

We also saw organized crime running rampant, with the paramilitaries and security forces deeply engaged. Crony capitalists who had propped up Milosevic had thrown their support to Djindjic, but their support came with a price. Corruption proliferated. To the average citizen who had voted for democracy and economic opportunity, it appeared nothing had changed. The same elements that had operated under Milosevic were rifling the economy.

On March 12, 2003, as I waited for Zoran Djindjic at the Hyatt Hotel, where he was to deliver a speech, a sniper assassinated him outside his office. Milorad Lukovic, former chief of the special operations police unit known as the "Red Berets" and leader of the Zemun organized crime group, had ordered his murder. It was later reported that Djindjic had, only days earlier, decided to arrest Lukovic and to begin cleaning up the problem that was strangling his administration.

Without Djindjic, his government atrophied. Several failed elections followed in which no party could win, because a majority of Serbs would not even vote. The radicals who had opposed the Djindjic reforms gained in power, and the government eventually elected repudiated his ambitious reform agenda. In 2006, Montenegro held a referendum and declared its independence.

Serbia was a painful lesson that the best minds, popular support for reform, and international assistance will not prevail if security is not given the same attention. Democracy, economic growth, and security are all interlinked and mutually supporting. Without domestic security, efforts to build democracy and create economic growth rarely succeed. Conversely, without civil society and economic growth, domestic security is difficult to maintain in other than an authoritarian state.

With this grounding I arrived in Iraq. In spite of the ambivalence of Jay Garner's Office of Reconstruction and Humanitarian

Assistance (ORHA), my predecessor, Lew Lucke, had designed and begun implementing a comprehensive stabilization and reconstruction program. Supporting him was an incredibly competent team of professionals who had worked in post-conflict transitions all over the world. One member was David Wall of International Resources Group (IRG). He was the de facto leader of our economic growth effort during and after my tenure. I have included in an appendix to this volume his written history of our efforts to create economic growth in Iraq and the obstacles within the CPA that had to be overcome to succeed. His account does not detail the obstacles encountered outside the Green Zone, our negotiations with a succession of Iraqi governments, or the personal travails of David's staff and the contractors who implemented the programs. I have included his report because it illustrates we knew what we were doing and fought tenaciously to prevail, often against the forces within the CPA.

5 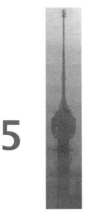 JONESTOWN

My first weeks in Baghdad were devoted to learning the details of our $2 billion program, meeting CPA and Iraqi counterparts, plugging holes in our staffing, and generally settling in. I soon learned that USAID was essentially an executing agency for the CPA, for which the Project Management Office managed the $18.4 billion supplemental appropriation for Iraq reconstruction and reported primarily to DOD.

The $18.4 billion fiscal year (FY) 2004 supplemental (Public Law 108-106, often referred to as "the 2207" after section 2207 of the law) essentially funded a list of large infrastructure projects in ten sectors. Adm. David Nash, in consultation with the senior advisers, had designed the program. An engineer who had once commanded the Navy's Seabees, Nash saw his task as overseeing the physical reconstruction of Iraq's dilapidated and destroyed infrastructure, such as roads, bridges, power, water, oil, communications, hospitals, and more. The nuances of stabilization and reconstruction—democratization, economic policy reform, private sector development, civil society, rule of law, community development, institutional support, and empowerment of local governance—were foreign to him. So, as he later said, he filled in "the blank sheet of paper" almost entirely with large infrastructure projects.

Given Ambassador Bremer's record of independent action, Congress limited the CPA's authority to make adjustments between sectors and subsectors or to delete or add projects. Even projects already contained in the 2207 had to be preapproved by the PMO, by the

CPA senior adviser within whose ministry or area of responsibility the project fell, by Ambassador Bremer, and, finally, by the Office of Management and Budget. This cumbersome and time-consuming procedure meant adding a new project could only be accomplished by canceling an existing one and notifying Congress.

I saw much that was lacking in the program dictated by the 2207, at both the strategic and tactical level. In particular, I was deeply concerned at the heavy concentration of large infrastructure projects that would be slow to develop, generate little employment, and be largely invisible to the average Iraqi in spite of CPA promises to the contrary. The whole approach ignored the lessons learned during a half century of foreign assistance, particularly with regard to post-conflict transitions. I found virtually no funding for reforms in agriculture, economic policy, health, education, public administration, or rule of law and inadequate funding for democracy activities across the board, including election support. In my judgment, the 2207 resembled the Point Four Program that the United States had implemented in the Middle East in the early 1950s, during the dawn of foreign aid. Point Four built large infrastructure projects there with little impact.

We were stymied by the CPA's structure in our efforts to make needed adjustments, by the difficulty of making changes to the 2207, and by the CPA leadership's conviction that the reconstruction effort was already on the right course. But we tried. With help from the leadership of the CPA's Governance Office, we were able to convince Bremer to put substantially more funding into democracy efforts, though the deteriorating situation in Iraq would require a doubling and redoubling of that amount.

Another point of contention was the BearingPoint contract. In 2003, USAID had contracted with this consulting firm to provide assistance in economic policy and private sector reform as well as technical assistance to Iraqi ministries. This kind of effort was common to the successful programs that we had implemented in Eastern Europe and Latin America to restructure command economies and promote economic growth. By the time I arrived in Iraq, however, the CPA had taken $35 million from the effort. Although we successfully fought to replenish this amount, the contract had largely become a technical assistance slush fund for the senior advisers' pet projects.

Economic restructuring is a nuanced and tightly sequenced effort that begins with macroeconomic reform and quickly moves to such endeavors as creating an independent central bank, bank supervision, and payments systems, and drafting laws to support a market-oriented economy. Unfortunately, the program had been hijacked by the CPA procedure that favored senior advisers' initiating task orders to BearingPoint. Instead of a cogent plan to reform the Iraqi economy and ministries, an ad hoc program based on the senior advisers' whims and interests had developed. Some programs, such as printing and issuing new currency, were necessary and successful, but others, such as creating a stock exchange and an economic council, were either premature or a waste of time and money. Some, such as running the food distribution program, though necessary, were costly and unsustainable. Moreover, by March 2004, the CPA had spent almost all the $79 million allocated to the BearingPoint contract, and we were facing the imminent termination of the entire effort.

That March, I approached David Wall of our economic growth office with a plan to bid a new contract. He agreed we would need new tools after the CPA's demise, but we had no funding. We approached Ambassador Bremer and expressed our intent to bid out two new contracts for economic governance and private sector development. He pointed out no funding was available, but he also recognized the contracts would not be awarded until after the CPA's termination. He agreed we could bid the contracts but left it up to us to find the funding. To me, David identified funding available for vocational training that was not and could not be used in the near term. The two of us cajoled and negotiated with the CPA personnel in charge of those funds and eventually obtained an agreement to "borrow" $40 million for our effort. We knew $20 million for each contract would barely permit the contractors to mobilize, but we were gambling that post-CPA there would be a realignment of funding by State and Congress. We proceeded to bid the two contracts in order to have them in place for the expected realignment. In the meantime, we found enough funding to keep BearingPoint working on worthwhile activities. Other activities were cut, infuriating senior advisers and sometimes infuriating Bremer. (After the Iraq Interim Government was established and the contracts were in place, we approached Deputy Prime Minister Barham Salih and worked out programs for policy reform, private sector development, and assistance to the Iraqi ministries based on our mutual knowledge of what was needed and what was doable in the circumstances.)

Under the CPA, however, we were not successful in obtaining any funds for agriculture, even though we were sitting in the Fertile Crescent and perhaps 30 percent of Iraqis depended on agriculture. We scraped together bits and pieces of funding to keep the contract alive until we could get more funding.

Like it or not, our flagship was a mammoth infrastructure program. In the run-up to the Iraq War., USAID had awarded a $680 million construction services contract to Bechtel and contracted with the Army Corps of Engineers to provide quality assurance and construction supervision. In the first months of the occupation, the CPA asked USAID and Bechtel to do more and more, and the contract subsequently increased to $1 billion. With the advent of the PMO, Bremer asked USAID to bid an additional construction services contract for $1.8 billion, which Bechtel also won. The express purpose of the latter contract was to "bridge" until the construction contracts being bid by the PMO could be awarded and the contractors mobilized. Thereafter, the PMO would be responsible for the bulk of construction.

USAID mobilized a small but talented infrastructure section that was supported by approximately forty engineers from the corps who worked in our offices or at construction sites. By January 2004, this group and Bechtel had completed or were constructing thousands of projects, large and small. Until the advent of the PMO, USAID had written its own task orders to Bechtel, enabling us to move quickly. Subsequently, the PMO issued task orders to USAID, and we in turn issued work orders to Bechtel. It became a tedious process. By March 2004, in spite of our repeated attempts to get more work, the PMO had issued only four task orders for $180 million. Robin Cleveland at OMB noted this paucity of work. She constantly harangued Admiral

Nash in telephone calls and, more publicly, in a weekly secure video teleconference (SVTC) on the reconstruction's progress.

DOD ran the SVTC and included the PMO, USAID, the Army Corps of Engineers, and perhaps fifty individuals from six agencies in Washington. It took place on Thursday evenings, with the Baghdad group crammed into a windowless room and staring at a wide-screen television and a video camera. Admiral Nash presided. The format aimed to update Washington on progress and enable participants at that end to ask questions. Robin Cleveland, under pressure to move funding from the Office of Management and Budget toward tangible results, hammered Admiral Nash on the PMO's progress and its slow movement of funds to USAID. Nash deflected the attacks without ever answering her questions. These sessions came close to an explosion but never quite reached ignition. For my part, I still was feeling my way, had to work with Nash and his staff, and was trying to effect a solution without an open breach. In telephone conversations with Robin, I asked for time to work through the problem, but Admiral Nash and his staff believed I was engaging in backchanneling and undermining his authority.

Our relationship with the PMO was becoming poisonous. By early March, the PMO had still not awarded any of its own construction contracts, and my engineers continued to press their engineers to issue more task orders. Then I began to receive reports the PMO did not intend to issue more task orders to USAID. Chris Milligan and I immediately confronted Admiral Nash and reminded him of the Bechtel contract's purpose. His response was to describe a grand design in which all work had to move ahead in unison, and he opined he might never fill the Bechtel contract. I told him, directly, his position was unacceptable, and he was forcing me to take up the matter with Bremer. Bechtel was already mobilized, and it would be months before his contractors would be mobilized. He shrugged and nodded that the meeting was over.

This conflict was more than just a turf battle. Fully mobilizing Bechtel to undertake $1.8 billion of construction was costly. Even if Bechtel was not working, its staff still had to be paid. More important, providing services—particularly water, electricity, and sewerage—was deemed vital to battling the insurgency, which was feeding on the frustrations of Iraqis who could not understand why a country that had put a man on the moon could not turn on the water and power.

I immediately met with Bremer. I recounted the history of acquiring the second Bechtel contract as a bridge at his request. I reminded him of his stated equation that infrastructure (essential services) equaled security and that security equaled saved lives. He responded Nash had promised to award PMO construction contracts in March and to be "turning dirt" by April. I explained construction contractors took months to mobilize. Then they had to receive work orders, design the projects, receive approval, and purchase and receive materials. Only after all these steps would construction begin. Thus they would not be "turning dirt" until September or October. Bechtel was already mobilized and just sitting, waiting for work from the PMO. Bremer responded, "Dave has thirty-five years of experience." I reminded him I had twenty-five years of experience, all of it overseas in post-conflict or conflict countries. Bremer's response was, "I'll go with whatever Dave says."

Astounded that Bremer would allow internal bickering to endanger the program most important to his success and essential to winning the war, I informed Washington of Bremer's decision. For the moment, I was stymied, but I knew Nash could not deliver on his promise and the game was not over. Pressure to show results would continue to grow; we would bide our time. Unfortunately, the war would not wait. The drumbeat of Iraqi dissatisfaction with the slow pace of reconstruction was constant, and it fueled the worsening insurgency.

Admiral Nash had designed the PMO's structure on a grand scale. With a core staff of more than a hundred 3161 temporary-hire civilians and uniformed military personnel, it contracted for seven program management contracts that would swell its ranks to some seven hundred people. The program management contractors would sit in the PMO and oversee ten construction contracts spread across sectors, with thousands of planned projects. Moreover, the PMO would control the CPA's purse strings, with even nonconstruction projects requiring PMO approval. The PMO not only decided who received funds; it was also the largest user of funds, resulting in an inherent conflict of interest.

The PMO staff was fanatically loyal to Admiral Nash. Perceived as interlopers, USAID personnel were reportedly referred to as "the tree huggers." Our engineers worked in our offices, offsite from the CPA in the Republican Palace. The PMO was housed at one end of the palace while it was renovating another entire building in the Green Zone to accommodate its growing staff. Going over to the PMO was painful, and my staff began to refer to it as "Jonestown." I sympathized—I also found it painful every time I ventured into the PMO or attended the SVTC—but we had to work with its staff. I never understood the origin of the enmity, which could not be attributed simply to competition. Others speculated it emanated from the Office of the Secretary of Defense (OSD), but there was no proof. I know only that it did not abate until Admiral Nash departed in September 2004.

The pressure on the PMO to "turn dirt" continued without respite, particularly after the insurgency erupted in April. The fault lay not in the program's execution but in the expectations that the PMO could do the impossible. Admiral Nash had made promises not only within the CPA but also throughout the provinces to hundreds of provincial council members and governors. In the meantime, we continued to wait for work.

In late March, Tom Gibb, Admiral Nash's deputy for programs, asked if he and I could meet alone and see if we could work things out. We met in the garden adjacent to the swimming pool behind the palace. He began by stating Admiral Nash was the finest man he had ever known and that he (Gibb) could not understand why we wanted to undermine Nash. He quoted Admiral Nash as saying no one had ever been as rude to him as I had been in the March meeting. Surely, we could all just get along and get the job done.

I reiterated that USAID had awarded a $1.8 billion construction contract and had mobilized hundreds of expensive expatriates who were now sitting around and waiting for work from the PMO. I said we ought to be the PMO's best friend, because with Bechtel already mobilized, we could immediately perform the bridging function we had been given. While USAID had no desire to be embroiled with the PMO, I could not sit idle for much longer and would have to start sending people home. I told him the solution was dead simple: "Fill the contract."

Gibb replied, "I give you my word that we are going to fill your contract." He then identified some work orders he was planning to give us, and we parted with a handshake. I believe Tom tried to be as good as his word, and more work did trickle our way; but our relationship with the PMO continued to be strained. Our people continued to call it "Jonestown."

One term used in emergency medicine is *the golden hour.* The military learned in Vietnam that if a wounded soldier received medical treatment at a field hospital within one hour, he would probably survive. In post-conflict transition terminology, the golden hour refers to the first year after the end of hostilities. Unless the population senses steadily improving conditions in that first year, popular support for change and whoever is in charge declines, and the chances for economic, political, and social transformation begin to evaporate, enabling recidivism and even insurgencies. Although events would somewhat improve our interaction with the PMO under its new management, that was months away. In the meantime, we were losing, or had already lost, Iraq's golden hour.

6 MUD WRESTLING

The transition from the ad hoc, temporary CPA to a U.S. embassy was fraught with almost insurmountable obstacles and had to be accomplished over a short four-month period. The CPA and its predecessor, the Office of Reconstruction and Humanitarian Assistance, which it had subsumed, were a reflection of the paradigm shift that occurred in Afghanistan. There, U.S. forces, the CIA, and their Afghan allies had defeated and ejected the Taliban in a matter of weeks. DOD then turned to the State Department and USAID, inviting them in to engage in the nation building that the military had hitherto eschewed. Neither State nor USAID were able to rapidly mobilize experienced officers in anything near the numbers required, and the military and DOD were forced to fill the vacuum.

Subsequently, when the planning for Iraq postwar reconstruction began—and, indeed, there was planning—it proceeded on two planes. At State, seventeen working groups with interagency, Iraqi, and expert participation met between July 2002 and April 2003 and developed a twelve hundred–page document called *The Future of Iraq Project.* Created at a cost of $5 million, it covered such areas as the justice system, local government, agriculture, media, education, and oil. During its prewar planning for the occupation, the administration almost wholly ignored the project's observations and recommendations. Soon after the invasion, though, CD-ROMs of the reports were sent to the Coalition Provisional Authority's staff. According to the website "The Memory Hole" (www.thememoryhole.org), the working groups foresaw, among other things, the widespread looting in the invasion's aftermath and warned against quickly disbanding the Iraqi Army.

DOD, having been stung by the failures of State and USAID in Afghanistan, went its own way. USAID did participate in ORHA planning, but ORHA management was much more concerned about humanitarian crises spawned by combat operations and gave short shrift to the long process of reconstruction. Hubris emanated from the Office of the Secretary of Defense, which ensured that DOD would be in charge of stabilization and reconstruction even though DOD had no viable plan for and no experience at either. The State Department's template for stabilization and reconstruction was ignored and rejected. The president could have cut through the debilitating interdepartmental warfare, but even as late as January 2004, with the CPA on borrowed time and the entire Iraq venture sliding south, he went against the recommendations of Congress and put DOD in charge of the $18.4 billion Iraq reconstruction program.

Against this history, it is not surprising that the CPA did not welcome with open arms the transition team led by Ambassador Frank Ricciardone and General Kicklighter. Although I am sure Bremer must have spoken to them at some point, he delegated the heavy lifting to Adm. (Ret.) Scott Redd and his support staff of primarily military officers. Admiral Redd was a decent, hardworking, and accomplished professional clearly tasked with keeping the CPA alive in spirit after its planned demise in June 2004. After leaving Iraq, he headed the National Counterterrorism Center.

My own part in the transition from the CPA to a U.S. embassy was both a paradox and a minefield. USAID administrator Andrew Natsios had tasked me with protecting USAID's equities while assisting a smooth transition, but I was also a senior manager in the CPA. As such, I sat not only in the negotiating sessions but also in the internal meetings of each side. I well remember a CPA meeting chaired by Admiral Redd for senior advisers were deeply concerned about what would happen to them when State took control. Early in the transition process, the CPA and DOD proposed the creation of the Iraq Reconstruction Management Office (IRMO). The plan was that the PMO would become a strictly temporary executing entity and be renamed the Project Contracting Office (PCO). Its overall program management and monitoring responsibilities, including the positions and responsibilities of the senior advisers and their staffs, would move to IRMO. Admiral Redd assuaged the senior advisers' concerns by stating the CPA would continue after State's takeover and its name would be IRMO.

The fireworks between the Washington and CPA transition teams began immediately. In the early phases, much of the debate centered on the need, or not, for IRMO, the shadow ministries, and senior advisers. The CPA was an entity of occupation; the embassy would be a diplomatic mission to a sovereign country. Embassies do not contain shadow ministries. Throughout a grueling afternoon session in a small, hot, second-floor room of the Republican Palace on the last day of the transition team's visit, Admiral Redd was effective and relentless. He would not agree to any plan that did not include IRMO, and he pounded away at the State members of the team until they acquiesced.

That night, I dined with Frank Ricciardone, who was visibly worn out and discouraged over this intransigence and hostility. Earlier I had seen an excellent State Department memo that laid out in detail why IRMO was unnecessary and should be rejected. The proposed IRMO's coordination and planning functions were adequately handled in U.S. embassies all over the world by their respective economic teams, which usually consisted of the economic counselor, commercial counselor, USAID mission director, and other officers as required. Advisers to the host government were civilians contracted by USAID, the Department of Justice, the Treasury Department, and other agencies as appropriate. These advisers were not U.S. government employees; instead, they answered directly to the agencies that contracted for their services. IRMO's advisers would be U.S. government employees, albeit temporary ones.

I asked Frank, in light of both his and State's opposition, why he had agreed to the creation of IRMO. His answer was that whatever we agreed to today would all change tomorrow or next month anyway. Frank was prescient in his analysis—things did change—but he was wrong about IRMO. It was created by National Security

Presidential Directive 36. After the transition, the ministry titles would be removed from the doors, but the hundreds of advisers, many of whom were capable of doing great damage, would remain.

Another issue was maintaining the regional offices, which were effective but expensive. State would be compelled to follow the security guidelines of the Bureau of Diplomatic Security (DS), and there was great concern about the field personnel's security and the costs of providing it. The CPA wanted State to keep all of the regional offices. In the end, State elected to maintain regional offices in Basra, Hillah, Mosul, and Kirkuk and to place a handful of officers at five military forward operating bases (FOBs). The rest of the regional offices would expire with the CPA.

Once the main points of contention were resolved, albeit not to universal satisfaction, the trench work of the transition began. More State officers, including James Jeffrey, began to arrive and address such issues as housing, security, vehicles, communications, records, and the disposition of the huge sums of monies the CPA managed or at least supposedly managed. It soon became apparent the CPA had no idea what it owned or where it had put it. For example, CPA personnel had been assigned some fifteen hundred vehicles, for which they had almost no records. Those who had been assigned vehicles had, upon departure, simply turned the keys over to someone else. The keys of a particular vehicle may have been turned over three or four times, and its location may have changed to one hundreds of miles away. Crammed four to a trailer, CPA employees often failed to report a roommate's departure in order to enjoy more space and privacy. Steve Browning, the highly competent embassy management counselor who had given up his ambassadorship in Malawi to serve in Iraq, once informed Deputy Secretary Armitage that he could not tell him what the embassy had inherited from the CPA—not how many vehicles, trailers, computers, or any other equipment—nor could he determine who or how many people were living in the Green Zone. The CPA left a mess that would take months to unravel.

USAID has always had a close, though sometimes rocky, relationship with State. In embassies, the USAID mission director reports to the ambassador and is a member of the country team. In the transition, we had the advantage of having been on the ground in Iraq for one year, and we would be staying. Moreover, the transition team had negotiated an agreement with the Iraqi Governing Council (IGC) to use a large residence in the Green Zone as the official chancery, and the Republican Palace would serve as its annex. The chancery was conjoined with the USAID compound in an area called the C-135. My staff worked closely with State representatives to install T-barriers, controlled access facilities, security cameras, and communications equipment for the C-135, often lending them our equipment and contractors.

State Department facilities overseas are designed and built under the auspices of its Office of Buildings Overseas (OBO). We worked closely with the OBO representative in Iraq at the C-135 and with regard to assigning facilities within the palace. When the OBO director, a retired army general, visited Baghdad early in the transition, he asked to visit our compound. We were in the midst of constructing hardened houses to accommodate our staff. For us, getting people out of trailers and into solid, safer, and more comfortable surroundings was an issue of security and morale. Each house had a living room–kitchen combination, a bedroom, hallway, and bathroom, with the last doubling as a reinforced safe room. They were built by Iraqi contractors and proved to be cheaper than the flimsy, dangerous trailers. Further, we could build them faster than we could obtain delivery of more trailers. The OBO representative, Alex Kurien, wanted his boss to see what we were doing and to make the case for doing the same for State employees. We had already offered Kurien the designs and the services of our construction contractors.

I met the general from OBO on the roof of the cafeteria we were constructing in our compound. From there he could see eighty houses, a sewage treatment plant, laundry, and other services under construction. We discussed the houses' lower cost, rapidity of construction, protection against rockets and mortars, boost to morale, and single-occupancy status. When he asked to see one of the completed houses, I showed him mine. He commented it was an "executive accommodation." I responded all of the houses, furniture, and creature comforts were identical. He returned to the cost and pointed out trailers were cheaper per capita because two individuals shared them. I replied that given the dangerous and stressful work environment, a hardened, safe space of one's own trumped any modest savings that would be gained from putting two people in a flimsy trailer. The general turned to Alex and the rest of the group and said, "We'll go with trailers."

At the time, OBO was planning to build a permanent embassy building and multistory staff housing that would be State's largest such facility in the world. The Iraqi Governing Council had demanded that the U.S. government give up the Republican Palace and other compounds within two years of receiving funding for the new embassy compound, and the general had promised to construct it in less than two years. But Congress had yet to approve the massive funding request. I will never know, but I suspected the general did not want to build the seemingly permanent hardened houses and thus inadvertently persuade Congress that his new embassy compound would be unnecessary.

This discussion was in March. April would prove the wisdom of having a hardened roof over our heads. Though most would not be completed until June, our little houses were to become the envy of the Green Zone. More than a few times stressed-out State officers called to plead with me to put them in one. One even tried to argue that we had assigned contractors houses and that State Department officers should have had priority.

Without question our hardened houses saved lives and made our people happier and more productive. I later discovered OBO's planned embassy compound would be designed to accommodate a "normal" embassy with dependents and not the vastly larger component that would occupy it when completed. This situation meant its staff would still be subjected to double and even triple occupancy until conditions in Iraq permitted a normal complement—whenever that happened to be. At this writing in 2007, it was still under construction, and most in the Green Zone were still living in unsafe, demoralizing conditions in the trailers.

7 THE MOTHER OF ALL APRILS

Three events in late March 2004 would have a profound effect on our lives in Iraq and on the American effort there.

It was my practice to arise at six o'clock in the morning, leave the compound by seven, and drive myself in an unarmored sport utility vehicle (SUV) to the palace. I parked in a crowded parking lot the size of a football field between the T-walled helipad, LZ Washington, and the palace. The lot did not have any security, and anyone could use it. Iraqi children sold chewing gum and black market DVDs to the stream of soldiers and civilians going in and out of the palace, which had little protection from T-walls. Soldiers did a rudimentary check for CPA identification at the palace gates. Off the main hallway, between the dome and the dining facility, USAID maintained a liaison office that was about the size of a large bedroom and housed four desks. It contained what could only be described as kitsch, with a collection of what was already there when the palace was occupied and a hodgepodge of scrounged furniture and carpets. Its air temperature was polar—winter and summer.

Arriving early gave me the opportunity to grab a cup of coffee and go through my e-mails on both the CPA and USAID nets. Baghdad was eight hours ahead of Washington, and though we often worked until midnight, each morning brought messages received throughout the night. The CPA never slept, and it behooved us to be prepared for the senior staff meeting at eight o'clock.

Following the staff meeting, I generally had breakfast with coworkers and went to the office to clear matters that needed immediate attention. I then returned to the parking lot, checked under the vehicle for explosive devices, and drove myself to the Convention Center. My third-floor corner office there had floor-to-ceiling windows of plastic sheeting and faced the general direction of the Tigris. Chris Milligan, my deputy, ran the operation at the Convention Center, which housed the bulk of our 120-member staff.

March 20, 2004, was a clear, sunny day. It was the kind of weather vacationers seek around the world. The day had begun very cool but had warmed by mid-morning. Teddy Bryan, who had been the controller in my Belgrade office, was due in from Amman on a one-year assignment to run the palace office, and I was looking forward to her arrival. At ten, I was at my desk, with my back to the plastic-sheeted windows, and talking with Chris, when a terrific explosion shook the building. The blast's pressure swept over us, rattling everything. One moment Chris was speaking to me, the next I saw only his heels as he crawled for the safety of the women's restroom. I was still sitting at my desk when my secretary, Seta Mekikjian, screamed at me to move to safety. I, too, crawled to the restroom, which was crowded with shaken colleagues. A single rocket, fired from across the river, had hit the newly installed T-walls just outside my office that guarded the road to the Convention Center.

The Green Zone had long been subject to sporadic indirect fire—rockets and mortars—but it had been inaccurate and infrequent. March 20 marked the beginning of a campaign of indirect fire and suicide bombings that would change the way we lived and prove deadly. That night, we were rattled by a rocket attack on the Sheraton Hotel, which was just across the river from our compound. Teddy Bryan, spending her first night in the Green Zone, rolled out of bed and onto the floor of her trailer. When she tried to crawl under the bed, she discovered it was a platform bed. She spent an hour on the floor, covered with her body armor and a mattress, not knowing if the explosions had been in the compound or if there would be more.

The second significant event was a March 28 meeting with the commander of the 1st Cavalry Division, Maj. Gen. Peter Chiarelli. The 1st Cav was deploying to Baghdad, replacing the division that had taken the city the year before, and his advance team had arranged our meeting weeks earlier. The meeting took place in our crowded little office in the palace.

Chiarelli arrived in full "battle rattle"—Kevlar helmet, body armor, pistol, handmade "CAV boots," and immaculate fatigues—and with a bevy of aides. I offered him coffee, and we sat facing each other in dilapidated chairs in front of my desk. He briefly explained the 1st Cav's mission and then came to the real point of our meeting. He believed reconstructing Baghdad and winning the Iraqis' hearts and minds were as important and central to his mission as securing the city and battling the insurgency. He was familiar with USAID and its abilities and wanted to form a dynamic partnership with us.

I was already deeply frustrated with the CPA and the difficulty of responding to events on the ground by not being able to make changes to the $18.4 billion program. While I welcomed Chiarelli's overture, I knew I was handcuffed by the CPA's structure. I could not see my way to the partnership that Chiarelli offered, but I did not want to stiff-arm him. My office had never been approached so directly by a senior commander. We were both cordial but exchanged little of substance. We parted with little intuition of how close our relationship would become.

The third event occurred on March 31. In Fallujah, an hour west of Baghdad, a Blackwater security detail of four men in two SUVs was ambushed and killed. A mob burned the vehicles, dragged the men's mutilated bodies through the streets, and hung two burned corpses from a bridge over the Euphrates. The horrific scene was captured on film and endlessly repeated on television. We knew the victims.

For weeks, our intelligence had indicated that the Muslim holiday, Arba'een, in early April would occasion increased violence and attacks against Coalition forces. At the same time, the Coalition authorities, tired of the rhetoric of the radical Shiite cleric Moktada al-Sadr, raided and closed his newspaper and drafted an order for his arrest. On April 4, elements of the 1st Cav were ambushed in Sadr City, a sprawling Shiite slum not far from the Green Zone. Eight soldiers were killed and seventy more wounded by al-Sadr's militia, which he had dubbed the Mahdi Army.

Fighting quickly spread to central Iraq and the Sunni Triangle. The CPA's regional offices in Al Kut and Najaf were besieged. Our contractors' offices in central Iraq were ransacked, and some of their staff members kidnapped. Others retreated inside CPA regional compounds. Supply convoys were attacked with impunity and burned, even on the BIAP road, and their drivers killed or captured. On a single day, eighty trucks that were the Coalition's lifeline were lost. Inside the Green Zone, increased indirect fire became a daily occurrence.

In Najaf, the Mahdi Army captured a small group of USAID contractor employees who were returning to their abandoned office to retrieve a list of Iraqi employees. The Iraqi employees were quickly released, but an expatriate was taken away. Teddy Bryan and I spent late nights at the palace working with operations to try to find him and to secure his release. The Mahdi Army held the man for three weeks before his release could be negotiated. His horrific ordeal may someday be made public—he was almost torn apart in the Imam Ali Mosque the first night of his capture—but not while fighting continues in Iraq and the Middle East.

While there at operations, we witnessed the desperate communications coming from besieged CPA compounds at Al Kut and Najaf, where our contractors had evacuated and then been trapped. On April 6, after three days of heavy fighting and with its defenders out of ammunition, Al Kut was abandoned. Najaf was hanging on by a thread. Fallujah was a no-go area, and Sadr City was the scene of daily battles between the 1st Cav and the Mahdi Army, with heavy casualties on both sides. One of our General Electric expatriates was killed in an ambush in southern Iraq, and all of our contractors and their Iraqi colleagues were at risk.

In the last days of March, I had asked Dana Eyre, a talented strategist who had lectured at West Point, to quietly investigate whether the CPA had an evacuation plan. Although it was a mandatory requirement in every U.S. embassy, no plan existed. So I asked Dana to develop a set of triggers to evaluate the worsening situation—triggers that would tell us when it was time to go. I had responsibility for the safety of more than a hundred expatriates, dozens of Iraqi employees, and three regional offices and indirect responsibility for more than 850 contractors spread across Iraq. When Chris, Dana, and I reviewed the triggers that Dana had devised, we saw we had already triggered three of the four. It was time for us to look after ourselves. Given the CPA's apparent indifference to the growing threat—the senior staff did not discuss it—I believed Bremer would explode if we planned for our own evacuation, but I also felt he would never order the unthinkable until it was too late.

I informed Washington of my concerns and about my office's work on developing an evacuation plan. My boss, Gordon West, was supportive and informed State, with an admonition to keep the knowledge "close-hold." Chris and I quickly formed a small group within the mission that initially met on a daily basis. We had five basic concerns:

- the safety of our people in the Green Zone;
- the safety of our offices in Irbil, Hillah, and Basra;
- supplies of food and water;
- the means to evacuate everyone from the Green Zone and our regional compounds; and
- the disposition of the 850 contractors not directly under our control.

Fernando Cossich, an extraordinarily competent administrative officer whom I had recruited out of an assignment to Colombia, had just arrived. A veteran of Bosnia, Kosovo, Montenegro, and Afghanistan, he was a master at building programs and facilities. Over the next weeks and months, his efforts would prove heroic.

I had never been comfortable with our offices in the Convention Center or with our staff living at diverse locations in the Green Zone. The Convention Center was a high-value target that could be seen from miles away, and it was close to the edge of the Green Zone. We knew from the transition process that we were eventually going to move to the palace as a DS requirement. An alarming number of rockets and mortars seemed to be targeting the villas, outside the compound, where many employees were housed, and Kroll had found what appeared to be markers near those bungalows where expatriates were quartered. After mortar attacks, the staff could hear Iraqis in nearby neighborhoods cheering, "Allahu akbar" (God is great).

We determined we would accelerate the housing construction at our compound; enclose the compound completely with T-walls; increase the static security provided by the Kroll Gurkhas to twenty-four hours a day, seven days a week (24/7); and establish better roving and static protection for the villas. As soon as new housing units were completed, we intended to move everyone into the hardened housing, convert the residential trailers to temporary offices, and abandon the villas and the Convention Center. Fernando Cossich increased our supplies of bottled water and emergency food and drove the process of rapidly enclosing the compound and completing the hardened houses. Our regional offices conducted their own reviews and upgraded their protection where necessary.

Kroll evaluated the capacity of our armored vehicles and determined they could move fifty-four people in one convoy to BIAP or a secondary location, where we would abandon the vehicles and all be airlifted out by Air Serv, our charter service. BIAP was the primary egress for Baghdad and for our staff and security from Hillah, sixty miles to the south. The regional offices in Irbil and Basra were close to the borders, and Kroll would drive their staffs to the nearest safe crossing point. We arranged for Air Serv to commit three aircraft to BIAP, on hours' notice, to fly us out of Iraq. The problem was we normally had eighty-five expatriates working in Baghdad and Hillah. I decided we would reduce our staff to the optimal number by sending some to work out of Amman, accelerating the rest-and-recuperation leaves of others, and limiting temporary duty assignments to Baghdad. We quietly reached our goal, which we maintained for several months. As we acquired more armored vehicles, we could maintain more personnel in-country, but we always stayed within the parameters of our evacuation plan.

Our 850 contractors worked for approximately fifty companies. We invited all chiefs of party to a meeting in the Green Zone, where we candidly assessed the situation and advised them the decision to draw down their numbers was theirs alone. I assured them they would not be punished for taking prudent precautions, and I would take any heat from the CPA. (It was soon too dangerous to risk the lives of fifty chiefs of party for a Green Zone meeting, and future communication was most often electronic.) By mid-April, our contractors had drawn down to essential expatriate staff, leaving only 150 in-country. The remainder evacuated to Amman and Kuwait City, where they continued to communicate with their Iraqi staffs by computer and cell phone. While our reconstruction efforts were slightly delayed, they were not slowed that much, and we discovered the projects with a large Iraqi component were affected the least. (Within six months, at our encouragement, the in-country expatriate presence of USAID contractors would level at approximately 350, while Iraqi staff increased exponentially.)

We kept our entire staff well informed of what we were doing and why. We listened to all suggestions, some of which were bizarre and others helpful. I made it a point to have frequent all-hands meetings with the expatriate staff to keep them up to date and to answer questions. For security reasons, we could not tell our Iraqi staff members everything, but we tried to minimize the substantial risks they took just to work with us. Once people understood the senior management group was looking out for them and making hard decisions, they were less rattled by the increasing indirect fire, the dangerous trips into the Red Zone, and the demands made of them.

During this period, I learned that despite my order that everyone had to vacate the Convention Center each evening by seven, several employees spent the nights there, erroneously believing it was safer than their trailers were. One evening, we heard seven explosions from its vicinity. Stephen Brager came on the radio net to advise that he had just exited the Convention Center and was taking shelter under the parking lot's overpass. I came on and asked if anyone remained in the center. He thought call sign Havana was still inside. Havana was one of those who had already been counseled about not sleeping in the Convention Center. My call sign was Gringo, and I immediately radioed Havana, who was indeed where he was not supposed to be. A terse exchange followed. I informed Havana to get out of the Convention Center and into his trailer in the compound immediately. The entire radio net heard us. The exchange between Havana and Gringo became one of those stories that was embellished and told again and again.

It was mid-June before we were able to abandon the Convention Center entirely. In the meantime, we had to move everyone from the villas into the compound after rocket attacks in those areas became too frequent and too accurate. Once the housing was complete and everyone was working and living in the compound, morale and productivity shot up. We were still working in vulnerable trailers, but Fernando Cossich installed laptops and satellite television in every house, enabling the staff to work from their hardened houses whenever they wished. At times we *ordered* them to work from their houses. After conducting emergency drills to locate all staff members and get them quickly back inside the compound, we restricted their movements, particularly after dark; established a shuttle system; and took away personally assigned vehicles that had permitted the staff to spread out all over the Green Zone and whereabouts unknown. Two-way radios became essential, and everyone learned how to use them.

We soon learned the downside to our cozy corner of the Green Zone. Whereas our corner had been remote when we originally chose it, we soon shared the neighborhood with the Ministry of Defense, the United Nations, and the homes of several high-ranking Iraqi government officials, not to mention the chancery. Communications towers—ours and those belonging to others—framed the compound like giant goal posts. Last, our location made us particularly vulnerable to mortars and rockets fired from across the river and the notorious Haifa Street. On one occasion, one of our Iraqi employees received a call from his mother, who lived near Haifa Street. She screamed at him to take cover as insurgents fired six mortar rounds outside her house. They hit around our compound a moment later.

April brought the start of a relentless pounding of our corner that would continue unabated for eight months. We put up T-walls inside the compound to shield vulnerable buildings and equipment, and they saved lives. Concrete "rocket boxes," into which we could dive if caught in the open, were positioned around the compound. For long periods, we wore full body armor whenever outside and picked routes from our offices to our quarters that permitted us to hug walls and dash for cover. During this period, USAID's Office of Transition Initiatives (OTI) offered to bring in a stress management team they had previously used elsewhere to good effect. It sounded as if it might help—it could not hurt—and I agreed. The stress management team got as far as Jordan and then refused to fly to Baghdad because it was "too stressful."

Most attacks occurred in the early morning or evening, but one of the most frightening occurred at midday. Sitting in the palace, we heard the steady explosion of rounds being deliberately walked across our corner of the Green Zone. We could even hear the launches. I was immediately on the phone to Chris, who shouted from the floor of his office trailer that they were really close and perhaps hitting the compound. But only one of that salvo hit inside the compound and where newly installed blast walls protected vulnerable trailers and the Gurkhas at our gate.

Soon after, I went to the compound to meet Bill Miller and a fellow regional security officer (RSO) to run a damage assessment. Teddy Bryan was not feeling well, and I gave her a ride. Four of us gathered in the driveway near one rocket's impact point and looked at mangled equipment and pockmarked walls and trailers. Teddy had just started for her quarters when more rockets began to impact close by. We had trained everyone to immediately hit the ground, lie flat, and stay there during these attacks. (Most people who are killed or wounded during rocket or mortar attacks are hit by shrapnel when they try to run for shelter.) Teddy hit the ground next to a T-wall and covered her head with her hands. I was forty feet away in the middle of the driveway. Both of us were lying in four inches of dust, ground to powder by the vehicle traffic. I could see small puffs of dust each time Teddy exhaled. Bill and another RSO ducked behind a T-wall. I glanced over at Teddy, just as Bill ran up, lifted her by the back of her shirt, and dragged her across the driveway to a rocket box. They made it, but Teddy protested the whole way. When the barrage lifted, we looked as though we had been rolled in flour.

A few nights later, a 107 mm rocket hit the compound. Many of us heard it impact, but the explosion was muted and sounded odd. A nighttime search of the compound revealed nothing, and we sounded the all clear. The next morning, the cleaning ladies found the impact. The rocket had hit on a steep trajectory between two back-to-back trailers. It had glanced off a small metal tower that held a satellite dish, gone through the tower's concrete base, and partially exploded underground. Chunks of concrete had been driven through Drew Parrell's trailer, but he was on leave. When the ordnance team removed the rocket, it was intact but had still opened like the petals of a flower. We would face closer calls.

As the April offensive worsened, it seemed business as usual at the CPA. The Mahdi Army was in control of much of south-central Iraq, and most of the Sunni Triangle was inflamed. The Marines attacked Fallujah and then were ordered to back off, creating the impression that the insurgents and foreign fighters were winning. USAID provided humanitarian assistance to refugees from Fallujah and other areas, and we knew the scope of the displacement. Convoys continued to be attacked with impunity, and supplies were dwindling. The fare in the Palace DFAC worsened and lessened by the day, which seemed to the denizens of the Green Zone a proxy measure of what was happening outside. Still, there was virtually no discussion of the problem in senior staff meetings. Rumors proliferated.

About the third week of April, Ambassador Bremer took his seat at the senior staff meeting and turned to Lt. Gen. (Ret.) Jeffrey Oster. An effective, likable, and well-respected administrator, Jeff had just replaced Admiral Redd, who had gone to an assignment in the United States. This morning, Bremer had clearly given Jeff a mission. Jeff cleared his throat. Then he opined there was much talk about running out of food, water, and supplies and even about drawdowns of personnel. He wanted to make it clear that supplies had been inventoried, and plenty of rations for prepared meals and back-up MREs (military meals-ready-to-eat) were available. The DFAC might not serve the usual three entrée selections, but we had plenty to eat. No one was to worry. Also, the Coalition Joint Task Force (CJTF-7) commander was now committing more resources to protecting the convoys (after a few initial setbacks), and the convoys and supplies would get through. Jeff repeated there was no problem. Management wanted the rumors to stop.

Bremer thanked Jeff and motioned down the table to Gen. Ricardo Sanchez, the Coalition's military commander. Until that point, I do not believe I had ever heard General Sanchez speak at a senior staff meeting and was surprised when he said (and I paraphrase), "If I have to maneuver, my priority is fuel, ammunition, spare parts, food, and water for my troops. Anything else is lower priority." There was a pregnant pause at the table, until Bremer said, "Thank you, General." Then he continued around the table. No one else said a word, and the meeting was adjourned.

Breakfast that morning consisted of a choice of hotdogs sliced horizontally or hotdogs sliced vertically. Fruit, bread, eggs, and other standards had disappeared days earlier. Lunch was MREs, which at least was convenient, as the DFAC had also run out of plastic forks and knives.

Our situation did improve shortly. Having poor food choices was never anything more than a minor inconvenience and nothing compared with what was happening outside the Green Zone.

The more poignant indicator was just outside our windows. Our palace office was directly beneath the flight path of the helicopter medevacs that brought the dead and wounded into the CSH. We could tell when significant Marine casualties happened in Fallujah, because they arrived by a gray-camouflaged CH-46 Sea Knight transport helicopter. A Cobra gunship escort would circle overhead until the Sea Knight had deposited its dead and wounded and could take off. Other casualties arrived by unarmed Army UH-60 Black Hawks. These medevacs were marked with a red cross. They flew without guns or armed escort, night and day. We said a prayer when we heard them lift off from the CSH and fly low over our compound to some battle. We could always tell when they were carrying the badly wounded, because they came in fast, flaring at the last minute to land their precious cargo. At times we counted ten in an hour. It broke our hearts.

8   KAFKA DIES HARD

One by-product of the transition to the embassy was a reality check on the worsening security situation. As more special agents arrived from State's Bureau of Diplomatic Security and realized they would be responsible for the security of an embassy of several thousand souls, their concerns mounted. I had served with RSO Bill Miller in Manila, and I knew other agents from my service in Lebanon and Serbia. DS has strict operating rules that run the gambit from U.S. missions' physical structures—they must adhere to the Inman standards—to the protection level of armored vehicles, convoy procedures, weapons, protective gear, and communications. (U.S. government facilities overseas are subject to strict construction standards to protect them from various forms of attack. Recommended by a commission chaired by Adm. Bobby Inman after the 1983 embassy bombings in Beirut, these standards are mandatory unless a waiver is granted.) Ambassadors must follow stringent requirements and conduct Emergency Action Committee (EAC) reviews periodically and in specific circumstances. The EAC consists of all agency heads and specific State Department representatives. Its deliberations and decisions must be cabled to the secretary of state. Ambassadors and RSOs are accountable for following security practices and implementing EAC recommendations. Decisions to draw down embassy staff or evacuate are usually initiated at the EAC and approved by the secretary of state.

The DS agents had never been thrust into a situation like ours in Iraq. We were standing up an embassy, to use the parlance, in circumstances under which anywhere else we would be standing down and evacuating. Although a wall in the lobby of the State Department honors all those employees who died in the line of duty, the department's general policy is zero tolerance for casualties. While Foreign Service officers are put in harm's way, State rigorously practices procedures to minimize injury and loss of life. Even in dangerous environments, embassies will draw down or evacuate when risks become too great. In Iraq, the policy to establish an embassy in a war zone dictated that the agents had to acquiesce to what their training and professionalism told them was unthinkable. Their frustration boiled over.

Following the debacle at Al Kut and the continuing instability of a number of CPA regional compounds, DS agents, supported by a number of us in other agencies, forced a review of the security status of each CPA outpost and the Green Zone. Primarily CPA military officers, presumably using intelligence from the field and from CJTF-7, conducted the initial review. At their first presentation, the highly respected CIA station chief was present. From the opening words, I watched him fidget, grow more and more impatient, and finally explode.

"Where the hell are you people getting your intel?" he asked with incredulity.

The presenting colonel answered, "We use various sources."

"What sources?"

"Various," he repeated, glancing around the room.

"Well, I don't know what you and your *various* sources are smoking, but your analysis is 180 degrees from ours, and you have no idea what you're talking about," retorted the station chief.

The meeting adjourned, with an admonition to the presenters to come back with a detailed analysis of each CPA regional office and the justification for that analysis. Bill Miller, Teddy Bryan, the station chief, and I adjourned outside the palace to talk, while three of us smoked. The station chief elaborated on his misgivings and offered some specific examples of what he considered to be whitewashing the facts on the ground. Miller agreed with him. I raised my concerns about the blinders the CPA wore, not only about the outposts but the Green Zone itself, and recounted the measures that we were taking on our own: instituting the drawdown, making improvements to the compound, increasing security forces, and setting up an evacuation plan. Both reassured me I was doing precisely the right thing and opined that we had to look after ourselves. During our conversation, I heard for the first time someone say the Green Zone was not green but, at best, "yellow." After first apologizing that she was a novice at security, Teddy expressed her apprehension that since our compound was on the river, a small force could easily cross the river at night and wreak havoc. The station chief replied that she should worry, for security had thwarted just such an attempt in the past week. We parted with promises to support each other and to continue trying to elicit honest analyses of our situation.

The next meeting, however, was even more contentious than the last. The CPA presenters had developed a matrix for each CPA compound, rating the critical elements: food supplies, water supplies, fuel supplies, threat level, threat type, communications, operational capability, and availability of a quick reaction force. (Mark Etherington, the British governorate coordinator who was forced to evacuate Al Kut, later commented that there was no "quick" in "quick reaction force.") Based on the analysis of these indicators, each CPA facility had been rated as Green, Yellow, or Red. It was never articulated, but we understood the colors to mean "relatively secure," "caution," and "cause for alarm," respectively. Even with this matrix, most of the facilities came out Green, which left the majority of us astonished. The presenters went back to the drawing board. At the next meeting, there were a few Green, a majority of Yellow, and a handful of Red facilities. We inquired about what plans were being made to evacuate the Red facilities and place a close watch on the Yellows. They answered that they were not making any plans to evacuate any facility. Clearly "operational capability" trumped all other concerns.

I asked the colonel who was presenting and defending the CPA position, "Let me get this straight. Are you telling us that as long as there is a single operative left alive on a base, with the ability to communicate to the outside, by whatever means, that the base is operational?"

"Yes, sir, that is about the size of it."

"So you have no intention of evacuating any of these bases?" asked DS.

"We can't," responded the colonel."

"Why not?" asked DS.

"Because we are in a war," responded the colonel, "and if we cut and run, we are going to lose! This is not like any other diplomatic posting, and DS cannot apply the same rules here that it applies in Norway. It's a war! Ask Mr. Stephenson how many USAID officers died in Vietnam. This is no different."

Although certainly some DS agents felt we had no business establishing an embassy in Iraq under the existing security conditions, most were simply following orders and trying to cope with rules and procedures designed for far less conflictive environments. Everyone in the CPA, and later the embassy, knew the risks—including death—and voluntarily accepted them. We were not risk averse, but those of us responsible for our people's well-being—and, yes, their lives—were committed to taking all possible measures to meet that responsibility. Our risk thresholds were not the same as those for soldiers, nor were we temporary employees looking for adventure. Our context was to do our jobs while reasonably minimizing the risks.

I tried to intervene with the colonel. I explained security is something one manages, as opposed to being managed by the security threat, but clearly the CPA would never countenance the voluntary evacuation of a facility. Still stinging from being driven from Al Kut and besieged at other compounds, the CPA had drawn a line in the sand. Neither fact nor reason would induce the CPA to retreat from that position. Though DS would continue to make inroads and our security arrangements would improve, the insurgents' methods would also improve. There was a butcher's bill to be paid.

9 THE BEGINNING OF A BEAUTIFUL FRIENDSHIP

The extraordinary events of April left me little time to further explore the partnership that Major General Chiarelli had offered, but at mid-month I was invited to a dinner in his honor at the Bechtel compound. Accompanying Major General Chiarelli were several of his senior staff members, most notably his engineer brigade commander, Col. Kendall Cox. With more than $1 billion in USAID construction contracts, Bechtel was one of our most important partners. Because of its numerous large construction projects in Baghdad, Bechtel depended on the 1st Cav to maintain a relatively permissive environment; however, a permissive environment was never achieved in Baghdad during my tenure in Iraq.

As was his custom, Cliff Mumm, the Bechtel chief of party, began the dinner with a PowerPoint presentation of Bechtel's program, which consisted primarily of large infrastructure projects. At about the fourth slide, an agitated Chiarelli interrupted the presentation.

He said (again, to paraphrase), "Just stop. Look, I know that Bechtel is an excellent company, and I am sure that the things you are doing are worthwhile, but you are never going to complete them unless I can get the sewage off the streets of Sadr City and get potable water into the houses of the people who live on those streets—because, unless that happens—fast—I am going to be run out of Baghdad and will not be able to protect you."

Around the table was stunned silence. Chiarelli then asked if he could put up some of his own slides and explain what he thought was needed. During the next half hour, he and Colonel Cox described a program that would concentrate on projects to install water and sewer pipes, restore electricity, remove solid waste, generate short-term employment, and immediately improve the lives of the population of eastern Baghdad.

General Chiarelli asked if some of the funds that were slated for large infrastructure projects in Baghdad could be redirected to electricity distribution, water distribution, and sewage collection. (The CPA reconstruction program counted on other donors or the Iraqi government to complete the distribution and house connections. An astounding gap in the $18.4 billion program had allowed the building of water treatment plants that had no distribution system, sewer treatment plants that had no collection system, and electricity generation plants that had no means of delivering power to homes.)

The central thrust of his plan was we needed to quickly demonstrate to the communities that we were engaged and that their lives were going to improve. The large projects could continue, but lives depended on redirecting funding to projects that people could see on their streets.

It was a studied and cogent presentation, describing a tactical approach that matched my own views about what we should be doing. My only reservation was he did not discuss the issue of community "buy-in," something we at USAID knew was critical to success. When I raised this point, Chiarelli's entire staff practically shouted, "We have it." They explained all the described activities had been either requested or vetted by neighborhood advisory councils and district advisory councils. My infrastructure lead, Tom Wheelock, Cliff Mumm, and I looked at each other across the table and nodded. We could make this work.

In the days that followed, Major General Chiarelli and I met and organized for my staff a full briefing by his staff at his Camp Victory headquarters. For many of my people, it was their first ride in a military helicopter and their first exposure to the U.S. military's extraordinary resources. We expanded Chiarelli's plan to incorporate other programs that we could tailor to our mutual needs, including private sector development programs designed to create economic growth and long-term employment. For his part, Chiarelli made available helicopters and ferried our staffs to the Brigade Combat Teams (BCT) to meet with the commanders and civil affairs staff. For my part, I impressed upon my staffers—many of whom had reservations about working closely with the military and had expressed that their partners also held strong views—the need to help the 1st Cav and the Iraqis by seizing the moment. Baghdad's obvious strategic importance justified such a concentrated effort.

Most were won over by the briefing at Camp Victory. Chiarelli and I then delegated design and implementation responsibility to teams working on various aspects of the program. Ken Cox drove the process for the 1st Cav.

The infrastructure team had identified $162 million of unfunded needs in water, sewerage, and electricity distribution. Funding the requirement would involve getting the CPA's approval to cut something else out of the 2207, and that meant going through the onerous process of obtaining the broad consensus of the PMO, the CPA senior advisers, Ambassador Bremer, and OMB. I felt the only way we would ever obtain consensus was if Ambassador Bremer basically mandated it, so I advised Chiarelli that he and I approach Ambassador Bremer directly. We agreed Chiarelli would make the same points he had made during the Bechtel dinner, and I would support him.

We had our meeting with Ambassador Bremer in early May. He enthusiastically supported our plans and directed the PMO to identify the funding. In the meantime, we brought both the PMO and the Army Corps of Engineers into the program, along with their construction contractors. The PMO eventually allocated funding for these projects. Admiral Nash was not happy about what some perceived to be an end run by Chiarelli and me, but with Bremer's support, we prevailed.

Major General Chiarelli initiated and chaired a weekly briefing, with all parties present, to track progress and deal with problems. It was called "The Pete Chiarelli Show." Colonel Cox organized and ran the meeting, but Chiarelli was in charge. A PowerPoint map of Baghdad was projected on a large screen, with graphics for every single project in the program—whether managed by the 1st Cav,

USAID, or PMO. Colonel Cox would summarize progress and problems and then call on the military officer assigned responsibility for tracking the project. Cox was a polite bulldog who was not afraid at times to tell Chiarelli and me to get out of his way so that he could do his job. We owed much of our success to his perseverance.

Chiarelli displayed an extraordinary command of the program, down to the minutiae of labor force and delivery of materials. While never abusive, he was demanding of anyone who was not moving fast enough—including, at times, my contractors. Inevitable friction occurred between the Army's style and desire to move at light speed and the civilian professionals with years of experience working in less developed, post-conflict environments, but we learned from each other.

One particular success was the contribution of USAID's Office of Transition Initiatives, which had been created to work in post-conflict transitions. In Iraq, Kirpatrick "Kirk" Day, its country director, provided extraordinary leadership. Day immediately grasped the need to put large numbers of Iraqi men to work and refined the mechanisms to do so anywhere in the country on just hours' notice. This capacity had tremendous appeal to the 1st Cav, which was trying to pry young men away from the insurgency with jobs. Thanks to OTI, USAID was able to commit to employing thirty thousand men in Baghdad alone, and at times we were employing even more.

The contractor and Iraqi subcontractors whom OTI hired took enormous risks, and the methodology they employed cannot be discussed here for their security. Working in the midst of an insurgency was a challenge. Workers were intimidated and sometimes killed and not always by the insurgents. Eight workers clearing trash at night to avoid traffic were mistaken for insurgents laying IEDs and killed by a mounted patrol of the 1st Cav. Kirk was furious, feeling that the patrol had been trigger-happy, but the answer to avoiding further tragic mistakes was better communication between OTI and the 1st Cav.

OTI became so closely integrated with 1st Cav planning that we requested and received a liaison officer (LNO), Capt. Dustin Felix, who worked, lived, and ate with us. After his orientation by OTI, Captain Felix said, "We [the 1st Cav] have no idea what you people

THE BEGINNING OF A BEAUTIFUL FRIENDSHIP

do or the scope of it." The LNO contributed enormously to communications and helped educate both sides to the limitations and capabilities of each. Through the LNO, OTI staffers were able to learn the "can do–roger that–make dirt fly–time now" culture of the military. Without this flexible, quick-response capability, the relationship with the 1st Cav would not have succeeded. By showing results quickly—more quickly in many cases than the 1st Cav expected or was even prepared for—we were able to gain the trust and confidence of the 1st Cav as a whole. Gaining this confidence and trust early on allowed USAID to put in place other mutually beneficial, workable arrangements for much-needed longer-term development. Given the contracting and engineering issues involved for the larger infrastructure projects, buying time was essential.

On the 1st Cav side, Colonel Cox was blunt: "OTI, as I have said numerous times, was an absolute lifesaver."

It was essential that Major General Chiarelli and I had a shared vision of what was needed in Baghdad and a political awareness that enabled us to assess the way ahead. More important was our firm conviction that our partnership had little place for egos or petty squabbling, neither with each other nor between our staffs, which we encouraged to work together at all levels. This association was often in marked contrast to our relationships with the rest of the Multi-National Forces Iraq (MNFI), which replaced CJTF-7 in July 2004. Some MNFI commanders either did not know what we did or thought that we worked for them. On one occasion, Chiarelli invited me to Camp Victory for a briefing of U.S. Central Command (CENTCOM) commander Gen. John Abizaid. During the briefing, I held my counsel while Chiarelli described our joint efforts. After the briefing, General Abizaid asked me if I was assigned to the 1st Cav. Clearly we had more educating to do before all fully understood our unique partnership.

The partnership with the 1st Cav showed immediate results in some areas of Baghdad, such as Al Rashid and Nine Nissan, by reducing violence levels, improving cooperation of the populace, and even increasing intelligence walk-ins. Meanwhile, other areas—for example, Sadr City, Najaf, Karbala, Fallujah, Samarra, and Tal Afar—were too unstable for reconstruction efforts and remained under the insurgents' sway. Nevertheless, MNFI recognized that "the 1st Cav model" held great promise in those cities if it could immediately employ its ideas after combat operations to make the cities secure.

At a meeting chaired by a British general I first learned MNFI wanted to replicate the model. The general was versed in its success, if not its most important elements. As he explained that MNFI wanted to use the model elsewhere, I noted the 1st Cav was not represented in the meeting. When I asked why its people were not there, the general explained because this was an MNFI operation, the 1st Cav did not need to be present. I disagreed but was rebuffed. The general explained the model would be first employed in Najaf and would involve close cooperation between MNFI and a multiagency civilian team deployed immediately after the successful conclusion of combat operations there. The Iraqi Interim Government (IIG), which UN envoy Lakdar Brahimi and Bremer handpicked, to supersede the Governing Council just prior to the handover of sovereignty, June 28, 2004, and would be a full partner. The IIG would use its resources to pay compensation for damage to homes and businesses caused by the combat operations. I was skeptical of the IIG's ability to move quickly on this critical element of the program. I also knew such a sudden strategic shift would require Herculean efforts to overcome the restrictive 2207. Nevertheless, the operation went forward immediately after successful combat assaults against the Mahdi Army in Najaf.

The team worked closely with local leaders and maneuver commanders to identify priorities, particularly those they could immediately address. Again, OTI's ability to quickly put large numbers of Iraqis to work, often at cleaning up the combat damage and removing accumulated solid waste, was critical. The model worked best in Najaf, Fallujah, and Sadr City once MNFI was able to establish a relatively secure environment and local leaders supported the effort. When the local population was convinced that the Coalition was there to provide security and improve their lives, security incidents and the insurgents' influence decreased rapidly.

In Samarra and Tal Afar, security was not sustained, and reconstruction efforts again stalled. Even where the tactic was successful, reliance on the Iraqi Interim Government and the central ministries to implement projects was misplaced. In particular, the IIG's slow response in making agreed compensation payments, which would enable the population to rebuild businesses and homes destroyed in the fighting, diminished the impact of the Coalition's rapid response. I had argued against relying on the IIG because I suspected that its lack of experience, its bureaucratic sclerosis, and its corruption would prevent rapid disbursement of compensation for destroyed homes and businesses. However, I understood the MNFI's desire to push the IIG to the front and demonstrate to the Iraqis that they had a viable and concerned government. It made sense on paper, but its implementation did not work well in the real world.

Pete Chiarelli is a thinking man's general who commands great respect and loyalty from his officers and soldiers. Most members of my staff developed lasting relationships with his troops, and many who had been initially skeptical about working with the military experienced an epiphany. Chiarelli's staff looked after us, even calling us to warn of imminent rocket attacks or to recall any vehicles we had in the Red Zone when there were specific and urgent intelligence reports of suicide bombers cruising for targets. The relationship, however, started at the top—with Pete and me.

Nothing better illustrated the nature of that relationship than a misunderstanding over funding. USAID had been expecting a task order from IRMO of $180 million to Bechtel for Baghdad construction. When the task order went instead to a PCO contractor, I was informed this change had occurred after Chiarelli, in an SVTC with the Department of Defense, had complained Bechtel was "inflexible." I was stunned, hurt, and icily angry. I asked Chiarelli to stop by my office in the palace. I prearranged for Teddy Bryan to take a walk when he arrived and not return until I called her. I did not want an audience for this meeting. He arrived with several aides, and Teddy dutifully excused herself (Teddy and Pete knew each other well. She kept him supplied with the cheroots they both smoked.) After offering coffee, I asked Pete if he would ask his aides to step outside for a few minutes. We then had a frank conversation, in which I vented my anger. Pete averred that he had not and never would complain about Bechtel or USAID in that manner. I believed him, and we cleared the air very quickly.

I called Teddy and told her she could rejoin us. When she entered the room, Chiarelli stood up and said to her, "Man! When you got up and left, I knew I was in for an ass chewing."

Obviously, there was no "ass chewing," but that response from a two-star general commanding 27,000 troops was a startling example of what an extraordinary individual Major General Chiarelli is and why our experiment worked so well. We clicked, and we respected each other. It was the most rewarding partnership of my career, and we have remained good friends. Pete returned to Fort Hood with the 1st Cav in early March 2005 but redeployed to Iraq as the Multi-National Coalition ground forces commander in January 2006.

10 EXIT STAGE LEFT—QUICKLY

As the June 30 demise of the CPA drew closer and the insurgency grew more virulent, the soldiers' epithet for the CPA, "Can't Produce Anything," appeared more and more accurate. By May, the Project Management Office's construction contractors were still not "turning dirt," and the decision was made to use funding from the Development Fund for Iraq (DFI) and what remained from the Oil-for-Food Program to contract directly with Iraqi construction firms in strategic—meaning highly conflicted—cities in the Sunni Triangle. Called the "Accelerated Iraq Reconstruction Program" and managed by the PMO, it did not have to follow the contracting rules required for using U.S. funds appropriated by Congress. Even so, little about the program proved to be accelerated. Instead, it drew away resources needed to get the PMO's contractors to actually construct something, and it was fertile ground for corruption. In the meantime, our Bechtel contract had ready human resources and capacity but only a dribble of task orders from the PMO.

Ambassador Bremer was heavily engaged with the Iraqi Governing Council in negotiating the Transitional Administrative Law (TAL), which would guide Iraq through the transition from occupation to full sovereignty. The TAL also established the schedule of elections and a constitutional referendum, and it would become the framework upon which the Iraqi constitution would be built. Bremer and a small staff of lawyers, political appointees, and seconded Foreign Service officers conducted most of this effort. Meghan O'Sullivan, Roman Martinez, and Scott Carpenter were reportedly

Bremer's closest advisers on the TAL. Great credit also belongs to Scott Castle, a military lawyer who ran the CPA General Counsel Office, and to a talented group of lawyers who drafted the CPA orders that were embodied in the TAL. Parts of the TAL were circulated for comment, but most of the CPA did not see the full document until it was published. Bremer would later write that it was his greatest legacy. Only time will tell, but he was probably correct.

During this same period, the process of turning over full authority to Iraqi ministries began. Until this point, CPA senior advisers and their staffs had exercised ultimate authority. In many cases, once sovereignty was returned to the Iraqis, they made it immediately clear the CPA advisers were no longer welcome. To some extent, this situation was also true regarding USAID contractors who were providing capacity building to the ministries, but in most cases our efforts actually improved.

Friction had always existed between the CPA advisers and USAID, and the situation often deteriorated into one of the groups working at cross-purposes. The return of Iraqi authority liberated the ministry staffs and resulted in closer working relationships between ministry personnel and our contractors, who (incorrectly) were perceived to be independent from the U.S. government and the CPA. Although fewer CPA advisers worked in the ministries, the friction and backbiting would continue well into the fall.

This period also saw a frenzied initiation of activities that used Development Fund for Iraq monies. The vehicle for this process was the Program Review Board (PRB). It had formerly approved funding for all activities, including those using U.S.-appropriated funding, but the PRB had evolved to approving only DFI-funded activities. PRB membership consisted of ten senior CPA personnel and two representatives from the Iraq Finance and Planning ministries. The board's decisions were advisory to Ambassador Bremer, who could act without board approval or overrule its decisions. USAID had a seat on the board, and Teddy Bryan performed that duty.

Between April 28 and May 12, 2004, $2.5 billion in activities were presented to the PRB for approval. Our first inkling that something odd was happening came with a rare visit from Sarah Horrigan.

Although officially from the CPA Ministry of Finance, Sarah worked closely with George Wolfe, the liaison with the Office of Management and Budget, who controlled the funding spigots. Teddy had received a CPA Funding Request to the PRB, dated April 23, for $500 million for "emerging security requirements." Sarah wanted to know how we were going to vote and implied by her unusual interest that we were expected to vote in the affirmative. Teddy was noncommittal but privately expressed her anger that her arm was being twisted. When the board met on April 28, the $500 million proposal was poorly supported by any description or details, but the board nevertheless approved the request. Teddy voted with the majority, but the whole affair left a bad taste in everyone's mouths.

In early May, I left for consultations in Washington. On May 7, Sarah Horrigan presented a CPA Funding Request to the PRB for $2 billion. Once again, the funding request was thin on detail. Before the board meeting, the member from the United Kingdom expressed great concern to us about the funding request. He and the Australians thought these monies should be preserved for the Iraqi Interim Government that would succeed the CPA. On May 10, George Wolfe sent out an e-mail in which he stated, "Bremer signed off on this proposal two days ago. MOST IMPORTANTLY, PLEASE DO NOT OPPOSE THIS PACKAGE AT THE PRB." The PRB met on May 12. The UK representative made a motion to defer and disaggregate the $2 billion request to allow for greater time and scrutiny. Seconded by the Australian representative, the motion carried by a vote of six to five. Teddy Bryan was the only American who voted to defer and disaggregate.

Bremer was furious.

I had been following these events from our offices in Washington but left on May 14 to visit my son in Charlotte, North Carolina. While driving, I received a call from Gordon West, who told me of an e-mail he received from Baghdad. Teddy Bryan and my deputy, Chris Milligan, had met with Bremer that same day and later e-mailed Gordon and me a summary of the meeting. The text follows:

Chris and I just came from the Bremer weekly. The PRB vote was forcefully discussed by Bremer. When Chris said that

George told him that Bremer was upset, Bremer said he was very upset and "don't do it again." Bremer said he cleared the proposal with the President. He further said that they had worked long and hard with the ministries, particularly electricity and oil. Those projects were taken right off the ministries' lists. When Chris brought up concerns (corruption/cronyism) on the Stabilization, Compensation and IPCC [Iraq Property Claims Commission] funds, Bremer dismissed them by saying, "That's political science, that's my concern not yours." He went on to say that "I'm in charge here, not USAID." Chris also mentioned that the proposals were not well coordinated and were poorly presented, which was the only thing with which Bremer agreed. Bremer said that the proposal was vital to U.S. foreign policy. Chris said that the national importance of the proposal was never mentioned to us, to which Bremer responded "I'm telling you now." Other items mentioned by Chris included:

- the concern over sustainability given the FY2005 20 percent cut in ministry budgets.
- lack of clarity on the $500 million security projects, which could change depending on the priority.
- the vote split between donors/GOI [Government of Iraq] and the military.
- the e-mail George sent prior to the PRB.
- the fact that the minutes and voting members are published on the web.
- the fact that the PRB advises Bremer and he could authorize any proposal without regard to the PRB's vote.

Bottom line, Bremer does not expect any USG [U.S. government] agency to vote against it. He actually directed us to vote yes (probably about a dozen times) and once said Chris would be on his way home if he didn't vote yes (he didn't know that I serve on the PRB now). It was a bloody five-minute discussion.

Spike...we really need to talk to you ASAP for guidance. Any feedback from USAID senior management?

Chris and I are buying our plane tickets out of here Monday. . . .

I told Gordon we had run out our string, and the earlier vote on May 12 would probably result in more detail in the next proposal. Nothing would be gained by our continued opposition other than Bremer's undying enmity. I asked USAID senior management to e-mail Chris instructions for Teddy to vote yes at the next PRB meeting. Chris received an e-mail from Gordon that said, "The Administrator instructs you to vote yes." When I next talked to Chris and Teddy, I directed them to save all of their correspondence on the matter.

On May 15, the PRB was presented with a disaggregated and more detailed request for the approval of the $2 billion package, which was approved. Teddy held her nose and voted yes, as Washington had instructed her to do. Our British and Australian colleagues still voted against it.

Bremer never mentioned the incident to me.

May ended, and most of our contractors and NGOs returned to Iraq but with smaller expatriate staffs. Our workload continued to be brutal, and the pace of transition to State Department control accelerated. Our compound continued to come together, and by the middle of June, we were able to begin moving everyone out of the trailers and into hardened houses. We abandoned our offices at the Convention Center and moved them into the vacated trailers. We continued to be subjected to sporadic rocket and mortar attacks, but having the hardened roofs over our heads lifted everyone's morale.

The advantages of a hardened roof were made painfully evident on the morning of June 13. Teddy and I had returned from the eight o'clock senior staff meeting, dropped off our things at the office, and gone to breakfast at the DFAC in one of Hussein's state reception rooms, a few meters down the hall. We were just sitting down with our trays when a terrific explosion and blast wave swept over us. Along with several hundred others, we dropped prone on the floor, among shouts of "Get down! Take cover!" I had secured what seemed a relatively safe position under the table when I felt someone pushing me out from under it. It was Teddy. Oblivious, she was trying to get as far under the table, from the other side, as she could. We shared the cramped space with eight others, as security agents screamed to stay down. Others pounded down the hallway toward our office to investigate the source of the explosion.

When we were finally given the all clear, we discovered a rocket had hit the cornice in the air shaft next to the dining facility and across the hall from our office. We also discovered work crews had been grinding the marble floors of the dining facility. Once again, we looked as though we had been rolled in flour. When we returned to the office, we found the windows had been blown open by the blast; everything was covered by the dust and plaster that had rained from the walls and ceiling. While we were surveying the damage, a suspicious backpack was discovered in the hallway near a window that had been blown inward. We were all evacuated while an ordnance disposal team investigated and finally decided to detonate it. It turned out to be full of underwear. An Iraqi officer had dropped the pack and fled when the rocket exploded. That evening, digital pictures of the rocket damage appeared on the Internet all over the world. Diplomatic Security issued an administrative notice asking CPA employees not to take electronic pictures and post them on the Internet, because then the insurgents would know precisely what they had hit. The explosion had been close, but no one had been seriously injured.

Three days later, during the morning of June 16, we heard a terrific explosion that seemed to come from across the river. I soon learned from DS that a convoy of GE subcontractors to Bechtel had been hit, probably by a vehicle-borne suicide bomber. Five passengers and an undetermined number of Iraqi bystanders had been killed. The survivors had taken shelter in nearby buildings and had been extracted by the 1st Cav. It was a heavy blow, because the workers were ours. This bloody attack signaled a significant spike in violence during this prelude to the return of Iraqi sovereignty and the end of the CPA. Rocket and mortar attacks on the Green Zone—particularly at our end of it—increased. On June 28, we learned another of our contractors had been killed when a single small-arms round pierced a

C-130 military transport as it was climbing out from BIAP. The contractor was one of only four passengers on the flight.

One thing we did not need at this time was a bizarre incident over the generators and magnetic security gates at the Convention Center. When the USAID mission had moved to the Convention Center in 2003, which was before my time, it had upgraded the chillers that cooled the building and had provided standby electric generating capacity. USAID had been asked to provide electrical generators for the Al Rashid Hotel, which it did because at that time the mission was residing in parts of the hotel. As the date for our move from the Convention Center to our compound approached, my executive officer, Fernando Cossich, advised the CPA Area Support Group (responsible for facilities in the Green Zone) that we intended to leave the generators and improved chillers at the Convention Center and planned on taking our generators from the Al Rashid Hotel to power the compound. (The CPA had purchased new generators for the Al Rashid but never installed them.) Incredibly, when our teams attempted to remove our magnetic security gates and generators, they were forcibly prevented from so doing. We were informed that the Area Support Group had determined the CPA owned all equipment—everything—of any agency considered a part of the CPA. Fernando was white hot and justifiably so. We needed that equipment for our own security and electrical power needs. Not only could the CPA not expropriate it, we were legally responsible for it. Eventually, the Area Support Group realized not only did we have title to the equipment but that indeed they already had replacements. We retrieved our equipment and installed it in the compound, but we had to wonder if we were all on the same side.

During this period, we significantly increased our staff of Iraqi nationals, referred to as Foreign Service nationals (FSNs). In 2003, the mission had hired a small staff of Iraqi nationals on one-year personal service contracts. When Fernando Cossich arrived, he immediately began the process of converting these employees to the more secure status of FSNs, meaning they became USAID employees with better employment protection. When hired, none of the employees had received mandated security checks, as the CPA did not have the capability to perform them. Now, Diplomatic Security had the assets to perform security checks, and Fernando submitted the names of all existing employees and all candidates for employment. As we were hiring up to more than a hundred people, it was a significant undertaking.

Six of our employees were denied employment clearances. One was a leader among the FSNs, worked in Fernando's office, and had access to all employees' records. She was an extremely competent and engaging individual from a prominent family. We were stunned. I went to Bill Miller, the regional security officer, asked if possibly there had been some mistake. Bill informed me she was as "bad as it gets" and was deeply suspected of being an agent working for the Baathist insurgents. There was no mistake. We were ordered to fire her immediately and have her escorted from the Green Zone. For months, she bombarded Fernando and me with e-mails protesting her innocence, but we had no recourse. I suspected Bill Miller was right about her.

I thought the summary firing of these six employees would have repercussions and that the rest of the employees would resent the security investigations. The truth was the FSNs were so suspicious of anyone outside their circle of family and friends whom they had known all their lives that they appreciated the investigations. It was just one more example of the legacy of having lived under Saddam Hussein. No one trusted anyone else. One misstep could end your life.

Violence continued to increase as the June 30 disbandment of the CPA and the advent of the sovereign Iraqi Interim Government approached. As we began to move staff members into hardened houses, it was brought to my attention that the move was causing a rift among our staff. In Iraq, our workforce consisted of USAID Foreign Service officers, who were career American employees; personal service contractors, or individuals on one-year contracts to the mission; third-country nationals who had worked for USAID in other countries and volunteered for duty in Iraq; Army Corps of Engineers personnel; Iraqi nationals; and, the largest contingent, employees of the International Resources Group, a company that had won a contract to provide personnel to the mission and our support office in Washington.

The IRG contract was initially viewed as a short-term expedient, until the USAID assignment process could fill all the expatriate positions; however, we were never able to fill all the positions designated for Foreign Service officers. Not enough people were willing to serve in Iraq, in spite of generous incentives.

In April, I also had precipitated a morale problem when I decided not to renew the contracts of a handful of IRG employees, some of whom had been with the mission for more than a year. Some referred to the day that we informed them of their status as "Black Easter." IRG replaced most of those affected staffers with highly qualified replacements, and the changes' negative impact was short lived. Tim Knight, IRG's vice president, had come out to Baghdad, and we had met with the remaining IRG employees to reassure them that there would be no further purges. We also dealt with issues of unequal treatment that had festered since before my time.

As the first houses were completed, in the climate of increased violence and indirect fire, a rumor started that our Foreign Service officers would have priority in selecting houses and would get to move in first. The truth was that Chris, Fernando, and I had devised a scoring system that factored in each person's time spent in-country and time remaining on the tour. We did not consider anyone's rank or nature of employment. Once we heard of the rumor, we scheduled an all-hands meeting, explained how the move schedule had been devised, and informed everyone when and where each would be moving. Not everyone was satisfied, but the morale problem evaporated. Once again, it was a lesson that stressed the need for constant communication and transparency, particularly when people are working fifteen hours a day, seven days a week, under dangerous and primitive conditions.

The houses, once occupied, brought about an incredible transformation among the staff. No longer spread over the Green Zone, we became a small village. Because people now had greater privacy in their own "place," they had more interest in doing things together. Small parties became routine, and people started various groups, ranging from poetry, to Bible study, to poker, to chorale, and to karaoke. Divisions dissipated, and we became more of a family, albeit with the dysfunctions one finds in any extended family.

To those who have never served in an environment such as that in Iraq, my preoccupation with my staff's safety and creature comforts might sound trivial, particularly given the proliferation of grossly exaggerated accounts of late-night parties at the pool behind the palace, steak and lobster dinners, and disco dancing at the Al Rashid bar. Most of us were simply too tired or uninterested in such activities. Admittedly, our lives in the Green Zone were vastly better than those of a Marine rifle team in Ramadi. (Actually, KBR served the same meals, including steak and lobster—which were awful—at military bases all over Iraq, and many large outposts enjoyed better food than what we had in the palace.) We were not soldiers. We were unarmed civilians in the middle of a shooting war. Without question, the Green Zone was safer than most places in Iraq, but it is not true that we holed up in the Green Zone and never ventured beyond its gates. We put convoys into the Red Zone every day, knowing the risks. Our contractors did the same. Too many of them never came back. An "oasis" such as the Green Zone was not a luxury. It was essential for getting the job done.

Morale in the palace was plummeting. All but four of the regional offices in the governorates were preparing to close, and many who worked in the palace had already decided to leave. Those who wanted to stay, numbering in the hundreds, did not even know if their positions would be continued at the new embassy, and if so, they did not know whether they would be the ones hired to fill those positions. Continued employment was not automatic. CPA employees who would make the transition to State Department employment had to reapply for their jobs and undergo security investigations. Not all would qualify, and great uncertainty prevailed. Hundreds were leaving in the last weeks of June, and senior managers were jockeying to be on the plane that would take Ambassador Bremer out on June 30. The logistics of safely getting people to BIAP, which was closed for security reasons leading up to the transition, were daunting. Some simply took the risk, drove their soft-skinned vehicles to BIAP, and left them there.

In the final days of June, I ran into Fouad Ajami, a scholar from Johns Hopkins University, as I was entering the palace. I was familiar with Ajami because of his prescient writings on the Middle East and descriptions of his observations in Thomas Friedman's incomparable *From Beirut to Jerusalem*. I had always admired him and took the opportunity to introduce myself and to invite him to stop by our office. He accepted, and we talked for over an hour. Although interested in what USAID was doing in Iraq, he was more interested in my observations about where the whole effort was going. I told him I thought we had probably lost our window of opportunity in Iraq. I expressed my fears that we would "settle for Egypt," or an authoritarian state with a façade of democracy that was allied to the United States but was devoid of pluralism and any real political voice for its millions of young men and women. Thus it could become the breeding ground for Al Qaeda and all the other violent Islamic fundamentalists. Ajami nodded his agreement and shared his concerns. Even then, I believe, we both suspected it could turn out even worse.

At the June 28 senior staff meeting we waited for Bremer to arrive, but he was uncharacteristically late. A much larger group than usual was in attendance. Teddy and I looked at each other. Something was up. Those seated bantered nervously. In the past days, the violence in Baghdad had reached a crescendo, and the uncertainty was affecting everyone. At about 8:10 AM, Bremer swept into the room with his most senior staff and aides.

Sitting down quickly, he announced that the decision had been made the night before to accelerate the handover to the IIG and end the CPA early to thwart the anticipated insurgent violence. The handover would occur that morning, and he would be leaving in a matter of hours. He thanked all of us for our service, stood up, and began to make his way to the door. Ambassador Dick Jones, Bremer's deputy, stood and began to hand out CPA commemorative coins. He finally had to resort to pitching them across the conference table.

It was over. Some were in tears. Most just stood around in stunned silence. Many would later lament that it was a shameful and unfitting end for the CPA. Within hours, a short handover ceremony to the IIG had been hastily completed, and Bremer had flown out of the country.

Most of those who had planned to leave with him on June 30 were suddenly stranded without titles, jobs, or transportation. The CPA had simply ceased to exist.

The State Department had decided earlier that Ambassador John D. Negroponte would not arrive until after the CPA's demise and Bremer's scheduled departure of June 30. Now, there was a scramble to get Negroponte into the country as quickly as possible, present his credentials to the new government, and inaugurate the new embassy. No one had apparently given him any advance notice that the CPA would end two days earlier than planned. Technically, we were all in limbo until he arrived and presented his credentials to the new government. On June 28, however, Negroponte was in Jordan, meeting with Jordanian officials. He was reportedly meeting with King Abdullah when he received the call that Bremer had left.

Late that afternoon, word quietly passed that Ambassador Negroponte would arrive later in the evening. Antonette Schroeder, a senior State Department administrative assistant and a friend, invited us to gather with what proved to be primarily State Department employees in the large room beneath the palace's blue dome. (Antonette had been the ambassador's secretary in Lebanon when I was mission director there. She and her husband Jeff, my close friends, were both assigned to Iraq. Jeff would later miraculously survive a direct rocket hit on his communications room on the palace's top floor.)

Negroponte, looking tired but ever the consummate diplomat, arrived at about eight o'clock. He was greeted by perhaps fifty members of his new staff and a few CPA veterans, who broke into spontaneous applause. Always cordial, he shook everyone's hand and said a few words, but there were no speeches and no fanfare. His only remarks were that we had a great deal of work to do and that we were now a United States embassy to a sovereign government. This gathering was followed, that night, by our first country team meeting. It was not long, as we used it primarily as an opportunity for introductions.

Teddy and I left the meeting and walked down halls that were strangely empty and quiet, as if all the CPA's lively action had been swept into another universe. After collecting our body armor and locking the office, we passed through the checkpoints and drove the darkened streets to our compound. We were under new management. The CPA was a historical footnote.

The embassy held a Fourth of July ceremony at the chancery. Though it was adjacent to our compound, most of us decided not to go. The chancery was clearly visible from the opposite bank of the Tigris, and most of us thought such a gathering was an open invitation for more rocket attacks, which we had been receiving almost daily. Security was heavy, and helicopter gunships raced around above the river and the chancery. Several explosions occurred during the ceremony and caused a momentary panic, but they were not close to the chancery. We breathed easier when the ceremony was over. That night, a Fourth of July party was held at the pool behind the palace. Many of the CPA departees were still stranded in the Green Zone, and the party reportedly went from nostalgic to wild. Few members of our staff attended.

Because of our workload, Teddy Bryan and I had a late supper at the Steel Dragons' dining facility. The Steel Dragons were a task force that provided convoy escort from the Green Zone. Most of the dinner crowd had departed, and we sat with two soldiers who had just returned from a patrol in Baghdad. They were both in their early twenties, exhausted, and filthy. Their day had not gone well, and they were still coming down from an adrenaline rush. Their experience was eerily familiar to me from Vietnam, but Teddy had never been so close to soldiers fresh from harm's way and was fascinated. At first, we just listened to them talk and unwind, but then we introduced ourselves and asked them about their unit and their duties. They were polite and seemed somewhat in awe of us. Soldiers did not have many opportunities to speak to civilian women, and they opened up to Teddy. We talked for about an hour, looked at pictures of their wives and kids, and shared experiences—mostly theirs. We were in awe of *them*. On our drive back to the compound, mortars started impacting around us. I could not tell where they were hitting and hesitated a second too long. Teddy screamed at me to stop. We piled out and crawled under the car until the barrage lifted. Other than scuffing our knees and hands, we were not injured. It rattled both of us, but the experience did not take the glow off the dinner we had with the two soldiers. That hour beat any Fourth of July party we could have attended.

11 ADULT SUPERVISION

Ambassador Negroponte immediately moved to distinguish the embassy from the CPA. Bremer's plane had barely landed in Washington before his suite of offices was demolished and converted into a conference room for country team meetings, which were scheduled four times a week. A country team normally consists of the ambassador, the deputy chief of mission, embassy section chiefs, including USAID, Department of Commerce, CIA, Defense, and any other important agencies. In Iraq, it also included representatives from Multi-National Force Iraq.

At the first scheduled meeting, Negroponte made it clear that the United States was no longer an occupying power, that there now existed a sovereign Iraqi Interim Government, and that we would comport ourselves accordingly. At one of Negroponte's first meetings, a well-known general embarked on a long monologue spiced with repetitions of "we have to" and "we must" with regard to strengthening the ministries of defense and interior. Calmly but forcefully, Negroponte clarified that we could advise and persuade, but Iraq was not "our" country. Our task was to help the Iraqis rebuild their country, not to do it for them. He sent a clear signal that our interaction with Iraqi government ministries and departments was going to be much less intrusive than it had been under the CPA.

The atmosphere within the palace began to change immediately. General Sanchez had ended his tour, and his replacement was Gen. George Casey. Prior to their deployment, Ambassador Negroponte and General Casey had agreed on their priorities in Iraq: security, democracy, and economic development. They considered themselves partners and recognized the need for close cooperation. General Casey began moving his headquarters from Camp Victory at BIAP to the Republican Palace. This relocation would take some months, as the palace simply did not have space for his 450-member staff until others moved out. The new Project Contracting Office, formerly the PMO, had been working for months on renovating another building in the Green Zone and was supposed to move there by September. At that time, we were supposed to move into part of the space the PCO had occupied in the palace. We knew the space was not large enough and suspected increased security restrictions for access to the palace would severely hamper the mobility of our one hundred Iraqi staff members and our reconstruction partners. We did not want to move.

Fernando Cossich was an expert at facilities construction, having built USAID facilities in Bosnia, Kosovo, and Montenegro. When we moved from the Convention Center to our compound, we had raised the possibility of building a permanent, Inman-compliant building there. We had been rebuffed by the CPA. Nevertheless, I had instructed Fernando to continue to explore the feasibility and cost of a building that would meet our needs. When we observed in August that the PCO was unlikely to move from the palace by September and General Casey's staff still needed room, I approached the deputy chief of mission, Ambassador Jeffrey, and the embassy management counselor, Ambassador Steve Browning. Steve was already tearing his hair out, trying to figure out where he was going to put everyone. I told them we could build an Inman-compliant building in our compound in four months. We already had the funding, and all we needed was their support and a cable to State from the embassy requesting permission. Both men were supportive, and in short order we had approval from Washington and began construction.

Fernando had designed the building as a concrete bunker with added features to protect against mortar, rocket, and small arms attacks. We had specified that the building would be windowless, and it was a measure of how little some in Washington understood conditions in Baghdad when they asked us why on earth we wanted to build a windowless building that might adversely affect morale. Our personnel, whose offices were in trailers, were elated that they would soon work in a bunker. We dubbed it "Fernando's Hideaway."

In mid-July, a team from Washington arrived in Baghdad for consultations with embassy personnel and the Iraqi Interim Government. On the team was Ambassador William B. Taylor. Bill and I had worked together when I was the mission director in Serbia and he was the State Department coordinator for the Balkans. Now he was being assigned to Iraq as the director of the Iraq Reconstruction Management Office, but he would not take over until September. In the meantime, Admiral Nash had been appointed as the interim director of both IRMO and the PMO's successor, the Project Contracting Office. Essentially, Nash was wearing two hats. As the director of IRMO, he was responsible for distributing funds to executing agencies, and as the PCO director, he received funds and ran that executing agency. This oddity was further complicated in that PCO reported to the Department of Defense and IRMO reported to Ambassador Negroponte and the State Department.

We all knew that a realignment of the $18.4 billion reconstruction program was badly needed and likely to be the new management's first priority. Negroponte, however, announced early on that he wanted to get his feet on the ground before tackling any funding realignment and reprogramming. Once he decided to begin the process, it was natural that it should be led by IRMO, but I wanted a fair and transparent system, particularly given our experience with the PMO and Admiral Nash. I received assurances from Bill Taylor that senior management was aware of our concerns and would ensure the process would be aboveboard.

Teddy and Fernando were inundated with meetings related to the transition from the CPA. They dubbed them "endless-loop" meetings, though they dealt with difficult and vexing issues. USAID had been on the ground in Iraq for fifteen months and had already encountered many of the problems that newly arrived State personnel now faced. The embassy management counselor, Steve Browning, welcomed advice and openly solicited the assistance that we were able to provide. The close working relationship we developed with

Steve and his staff boosted our morale and was a salutary improvement over our strained relationship with the Area Support Group under the CPA. Steve also appreciated that we were largely self-sufficient—we had our own housing, offices, security, operating funds, power, transportation, and operating rules—and he did not have to worry about us. We did our best to assist him in any way we could.

As Steve wrestled with the administrative mess left by the CPA, some of the requests he encountered were bizarre. For instance, the CPA had stacked sandbag revetments around the Green Zone's hundreds of housing trailers and other facilities. Unfortunately, the material from which the sandbags were constructed was not resistant to ultraviolet light and promptly deteriorated in Baghdad's bright sunlight and heat. The revetments were beginning to look like cakes left out in the rain. Various fixes, including spraying the escaping sand with glue, had been tried but to no avail. Steve announced every agency would have to provide expatriates to supervise gangs of Iraqi laborers, who would fill new sandbags and rebuild the revetments. My immediate reaction was it was not a good use of highly paid expatriates, and Teddy pointed out it was not a good idea to have unarmed expatriates, particularly women, supervise gangs of Iraqi laborers. Eventually, Gurkhas were assigned the supervisory responsibility, but it took months to rebuild the revetments.

Embedded in our compound was a fusion cell of several highly experienced intelligence analysts from Kroll who prepared a daily security report and a more restricted monthly security assessment. The daily report was disseminated by e-mail to a large list that included members of Congress and other Washington officials, but its primary users were our partners and other parties in Iraq. Everyone in our operation read the reports. Even when the analyses were frightening, knowing that someone was looking out for us reassured everyone. The reports were tools we used to reduce our risks, even if we could do nothing about the threat. Occasionally, political analysis and opinion crept into the daily reports, much to Washington's distress. After repeatedly cautioning Kroll to rein in their authors, I finally resorted to removing USAID's name from the report's heading and calling it the "Kroll Daily Report." Still, I would receive calls in

"Route Irish," the road to Baghdad International Airport—the deadliest road in the world. Fernando Cossich

Everyone walked away from this USAID armored vehicle destroyed by a suicide car bomber on the infamous BIAP road in December 2004. Chris Milligan

USAID mission director Spike Stephenson (left), with a Kroll bodyguard and the Bechtel project manager, on a visit to the Taza power station near Kirkuk in northern Iraq in March 2004. USAID

Fernando Cossich (right), USAID/Iraq's executive officer, on his way to Irbil in full body armor. His efforts to protect his staff were heroic. Collection of Fernando Cossich

The USAID compound under construction in May 2004. The dates, one week apart, indicate the rapid pace of construction. Fernando Cossich

Rocket shrapnel failed to penetrate one of the USAID hard houses in August 2004. Fernando Cossich

Teddy Bryan, USAID/Iraq program officer, in "full battle rattle" about to board a helicopter for Camp Victory in May 2004. Collection of Teddy Bryan

Col. Kendall Cox, commander of the 1st Cavalry Division's engineer brigade, meets with a Baghdad official. Collection of Kendall Cox

Maj. Gen. Peter Chiarelli, USA, the brilliant commander of the 1st Cavalry Division, who knew that projects to improve the Iraqis' lives were more important than bullets. Erin Chiarelli

Kirkpatrick Day (fourth from left), country director of USAID's Office of Transition Initiatives, visits with displaced Kurds in Irbil. Collection of Kirk Day

A USAID armored vehicle attacked in May 2004 en route to a Bechtel construction site. No one was injured. Fernando Cossich

Chris Milligan, USAID deputy director, visits an infrastructure project.
Collection of Chris Milligan

The author gives an interview to Army Times *reporters at the inauguration of
the Tikrit Bridge in September 2004.* Teddy Bryan

The author says farewell in March 2005 to Major General Chiarelli days before each departed Iraq. USAID

Chris Milligan (left) and the author present a certificate of appreciation to Allyson Stroschein at a farewell ceremony in March 2005. Collection of Chris Milligan

the middle of the night from my masters in Washington, who would complain about some item gleaned from the report, particularly if it remotely questioned or critiqued administration policy. I thought these reactions were petty and illustrative of Washington's indifference to our reality. We tried to restrict the report's distribution, but immediately we received outraged complaints from congressional staffers and Washington bureaucrats who demanded reinstatement to the recipient list. We never came up with a satisfactory solution, but at least we continued to publish the valuable report.

Shortly after Ambassador Negroponte's arrival, he asked me to accompany him to Basra, where he would formally inaugurate the Regional Embassy Office, meet with local leaders and the British contingent, and visit some USAID projects. We departed at dawn in two Black Hawk helicopters with two AH-64 Apache helicopter escorts, flying at treetop level. We landed at Al Kut for what was supposed to be a twenty-minute refueling stop. Unfortunately, the Ukrainian contingent based there was not expecting us and first had to refuel the fuel truck. While we waited, I talked to the Apache pilots. Both had taken part in the ill-fated attack on central Iraq–based air defense facilities during the drive on Baghdad, when an AH-64 Apache helicopter had been shot down and its pilots captured. Their story was harrowing. Virtually every one of the thirty-odd Apaches that participated in the battle had sustained damage. The two pilots I talked to had returned to Kuwait with all their communications devices and instruments shot away, leaving them to navigate home with a handheld compass.

As we flew south in 120-degree heat, the inside of the Black Hawk turned into an oven. In our Kevlar helmets and body armor, we got a good feel for what soldiers experienced every day. Once we landed at the Basra Regional Office, Negroponte changed into a suit for the dedication ceremony. By this time, it was 130 degrees, and I felt for him. Standing in the open, his suit was immediately soaked with perspiration. I was wearing khakis and a polo shirt, searching for shade, and was still miserable.

At our luncheon with local authorities, they pilloried the central government and pleaded for more autonomy over their own affairs. I had heard the same pleas in Kurdistan, but Saddam Hussein's government had particularly neglected Shiite Basra, and little had changed. One of their most urgent needs was clean water, and they were grateful to hear we were working on the problem. We left the luncheon and flew to the British base at the Basra Airport. There, we piled into a convoy and visited the terminus of the Sweetwater Canal, which supplied all of Basra's water. Bechtel had just completed extensive repairs to the canal and rehabilitated the main pumping station, which we also visited. We still needed to replace the entire distribution system in Basra, but a lack of security was slowing our efforts.

While Negroponte met with the British military commander, I took the opportunity to visit USAID's regional office on the base and to meet with those Iraqis who were implementing the community action program. Highly successful, the program worked at the community level to provide basic services, jobs, and increased incomes. It was driven by community action groups and, in spite of the insurgency, was successful all over Iraq. I had seen in other countries how small infusions of funding and local empowerment could be effective, and in Iraq it was no different. Tom Staal, our regional coordinator, had lived in Basra as a child and knew what he was doing. It was my first and last visit to Basra, and my time there was all too short. Late in the afternoon, we boarded a C-130 transport and flew back to BIAP. Waiting helicopters returned us to the Green Zone.

I had always been concerned that since State had decided to house its personnel in trailers, our hardened houses would cause friction. Now we had received permission to construct a protected office building, and we were also constructing a cafeteria on the compound we shared with the chancery. Embassies around the world make every effort to ensure that housing for their staff is adequate and fairly equal in size and quality. Clearly, our staff was better housed and, when the cafeteria was operational, would be better fed. Personnel in the Green Zone ate at dining facilities operating under DOD contract with Kellogg, Brown and Root. While the food was usually plentiful and nourishing, people tired of bland cafeteria fare, plastic plates, and plastic tableware. Our cafeteria would have better food, porcelain plates, glassware, and stainless tableware. Permission for the cafeteria had been granted because security concerns were making it increasingly difficult for our Iraqi nationals to gain entry to any of the DFACs. Further, the increased threat of indirect fire militated against unnecessary movement, and the route to the DFAC closest to our compound had been repeatedly hit. Several of our people had narrowly avoided being killed by mortar fire, and many started eating MREs in their houses rather than risk the gauntlet to the Steel Dragons' DFAC. Our houses, the office bunker, and the cafeteria made good sense, but I knew they were going to cause problems outside the compound.

Most embassy personnel worked in the palace, but about thirty worked in the chancery. While we could not open our compound and cafeteria to everyone who wanted to eat there—it simply did not have the capacity, and we could not legitimately fund such an operation— we could feed the chancery employees. I approached Steve Browning with the offer to provide meals to the chancery group and a reasonable number of guests who might be visiting the chancery during working hours. Our plan was to provide employees identity (ID) cards to gain entry to the cafeteria, and I asked Steve for a list of chancery employees. Through no fault of Steve's, the first list we received had double the number of employees who worked in the chancery. In the end, Steve and I whittled down the list to those who actually worked there and added a reasonable number of visitor ID cards. We had a gentleman's agreement that I would accommodate legitimate surges, and Steve would ensure that we would not be overwhelmed. It worked, but as our compound and cafeteria became the envy of the Green Zone, I understood the resentment that some felt.

I forgot my concerns when the cafeteria finally opened, and we saw how much food our Iraqi staff routinely ate. They were loading up while at work, so their families at home would have one less mouth to feed. It was another lesson that no matter how hard our lives in the Green Zone might seem at times, life was infinitely harder for the Iraqis.

12 | TRENCH WARFARE

Understandably, Ambassador Negroponte wanted to get his feet on the ground before initiating the process of realigning the $18.4 billion program that had become the State Department's responsibility. But the deteriorating situation on the ground and pressures from Washington dictated a rapid review and subsequent decisions to redirect the program. Effectively this new focus meant canceling infrastructure projects worth billions of dollars and reprogramming the savings into other projects deemed more in line with the objectives of helping Iraq become secure and democratic and of establishing a viable economy. Although USAID was managing more than $2 billion in infrastructure projects, we believed the Iraq program was too heavily skewed to building infrastructure at the expense of assistance in health, education, agriculture, economic policy reform, private sector development, and building democracy, capacity, and civil society. Many in the Iraq Reconstruction Management Office and the Project Contracting Office were committed to the Iraq program as designed and wanted as little change as possible. The Iraqis themselves were divided and often confused by what they saw as fickle behavior on our part. The realignment process quickly evolved into a battle between USAID and State on the side of changing to more transformational assistance and IRMO and PCO on the side of the status quo. The battle was fought in July.

My staff and I had positioned our program so that we had contractors and NGOs on the ground who were able to immediately expand their activities in all the areas for which we were seeking additional funding. We had also gained credibility with our successful 1st Cav partnership and with the Office of Transition Initiative's ability to employ large numbers of Iraqis. PCO was at a disadvantage because most of its infrastructure projects were not yet under construction, and the pressure from Washington to see results was relentless. Still, Admiral Nash and IRMO, which then consisted mostly of individuals who had been administratively moved from PCO to IRMO, would fight to keep the construction program that Nash had designed and was trying to implement. It was hard to tell where PCO ended and IRMO began or vice versa.

Chris Milligan and Allyson Stroschein volunteered to lead our effort in the realignment. We had already had each of our offices prepare a request for additional funding with justifications. In sum, we were seeking an additional $1.2 billion. IRMO placed Allen Zeman in charge of the review process, which was torturous. Demands for data were constant and taxing and were followed by endless meetings and still more requests for data. It was not uncommon to meet with IRMO at the palace until midnight and then be required to provide new materials by eight the following morning. Chris and Allyson basically ran a command center, delegating the demand for information to appropriate offices, collating and preparing presentations, and assigning presenters. It was a finely tuned machine, but maintaining it was exhausting. The process went on for weeks. My role, by plan, was to be brought in only when aggressive offense or defense was required at my level. We knew we had to survive an onerous and contentious process with our requested increase in funding intact. Zeman was not an impartial interlocutor, and we constantly felt as if we were swimming upstream. However, IRMO was only a facilitator. John Negroponte and a few of his advisers would make the final decision regarding our request. Ultimately, the committee of cabinet deputy secretaries in Washington would have to ratify it, but Ambassador Negroponte's nod was critical. We needed to be sure that I and not IRMO would present our request to Negroponte.

The military's initial request for funding was modest, but midway through the review process, Lt. Gen. David Petraeus, who had recently returned to Iraq to rebuild the Iraqi Army and security forces, presented a compelling request for several billion dollars. It was immediately apparent that though he might not receive everything he was asking for right away, security was such a critical problem he would get much of it. Our task had just become exponentially more difficult.

The realignment exercise culminated in presentations by the executing agencies, the military, and several senior advisers who were arguing for reallocations to their respective ministries. Ambassador Negroponte and General Casey chaired the meeting, which was held in a large, second-floor conference room in the palace. We were required to provide our presentations in advance, in PowerPoint, to Allen Zeman. PCO's report consisted of almost sixty slides and essentially defended the existing program—the status quo—and offered an assessment of the damage that would be done by changing course. The case I presented was a seven-slide piece entitled "Comprehensive Development." I began:

> If we do not improve the capacity of the Iraqi Government to govern justly and provide services to its citizens, if we do not create the enabling environment for economic growth and political pluralism, I fear that at the end of the day we will leave Iraq—albeit with the best-trained security forces and infrastructure in the region—with another authoritarian government, and we will have failed. We will have failed because that is not the liberal democracy with a free-market economy that Secretary Colin Powell promised the Iraqi people. We will have failed the Iraqis, the American taxpayers, and ourselves—and all the blood and money will have been for nothing.

Our presentation described the integrated program we wanted to implement and the impact it could have. We asked for more funding for agriculture, community development, economic policy reform, private sector growth and restructuring, civil society, parliamentary assistance, election support, rule of law, capacity building, health, education, democracy building, and stabilization through the various

OTI programs. The presentation lasted fifteen minutes, followed by questions, many of which pertained to how quickly we could start. The spadework we had been doing for months now paid off. For every element of the program, we already had boots on the ground. We lacked only the additional funding. With it, we could expand immediately.

I knew that we had scored, but the billions that Lt. Gen. Petraeus needed were going to cut severely into our request for $1.2 billion. We only had to wait for the deliberations of Ambassador Negroponte and his advisers. Within a few days, word leaked out they had prepared a draft list of approved and rejected USAID requests. I soon obtained a bootleg copy. New funding for rule of law, health, and education had been rejected, as had funding for our successful community action program. The logic behind these rejections was that these programs either did not need immediate funding or were considered less "vital" during the coming year. Originally, $100 million for agriculture was off the list but was approved after Negroponte visited the minister of agriculture, who had been brilliantly prepared by Jonathan Greenham, our British agriculture officer. In all, we received $755 million in new funding, and there would be more to come. By the end of the year, the USAID program had swelled to $5.1 billion.

We were elated, but we knew that Iraqi ministers and local governments would protest bitterly after learning their promised water and electricity projects would now be canceled. Electricity and water were the largest sectors and would have to take the largest cuts. Since our infrastructure projects with Bechtel were almost all under construction, PCO took almost all of the cuts and was, understandably, not happy. Much of the burden of breaking the news to the affected ministers fell on Admiral Nash and his replacement, Bill Taylor. It was not a task that anyone envied. It had to have been particularly galling for Admiral Nash, who had designed the program he was now being forced to partially dismantle.

13 | THE OUTCOME STILL IN DOUBT

In mid-July, I received a call from one member of a small advisory group that had arrived with Ambassador Negroponte. He explained he was working with Maj. Gen. Hank Stratman, who at General Casey's instruction had set up a section named "Political/ Military/Economic" (PME). The caller requested that Kirk Day, the country director of our Office of Transition Initiatives, and I meet with them. He didn't provide any other information about the meeting.

Kirk and I had earlier accompanied the ambassador and the same adviser to a briefing at the 1st Cav, 5th Brigade Combat Team at its base in Al Rashid, a southern district of Baghdad. Col. Steve Lanza, the 5th BCT commander, was highly committed to the partnership between USAID and the 1st Cav. At the briefing, he extolled the success of emphasizing small reconstruction projects such as those the 5th BCT was implementing with the assistance of local communities and leaders. He backed it up with statistics showing a significant drop in insurgent attacks and an exponential increase in intelligence received from Iraqis that had resulted in the discovery of weapons caches and bomb-making factories. Colonel Lanza and Major General Chiarelli had high praise for USAID and OTI. Thus, I suspected the requested meeting with the adviser and Major General Stratman had something to do with our partnership with the 1st Cav.

The meeting was held in a windowless room in the palace, where the adviser greeted us warmly and introduced us to Hank Stratman and a senior operative from the "other government agency" (OGA), which was a euphemism for the CIA or other intelligence services.

The adviser quickly explained the group had been assigned the task of analyzing how we could win the war with a better-integrated military campaign and reconstruction program. They wanted our ideas but seemed particularly fascinated with the USAID–1st Cav program and why it worked. At this time, we were in the throes of realigning the $18.4 billion program, so I welcomed the opportunity to engage them without having to resort to a PowerPoint presentation.

I explained our view that the reconstruction program was deeply flawed. We believed stabilization and reconstruction required putting a heavy presence on the ground, initiating and quickly completing small projects in basic infrastructure, and generating employment that involves the community and demonstrates change and improvement. The Iraq reconstruction program had essentially been a construction program with a concentration on large infrastructure, such as roads, bridges, electricity generation, water and sewer plants, airports, and ports. I said, "It may be that we are building a water treatment plant only a few miles from Sadr City, but that means nothing to a resident of Sadr City who has no running water and has to wade through standing sewage to look for work. There is nothing inherently wrong with building the water treatment plant, but it is invisible, capital intensive, and takes several years to complete. On the other hand, pumping off the standing sewage, delivering water by tanker truck, picking up solid waste, and, most important, trenching and laying the pipes for sewerage and potable water in the community employs large numbers of young men, instills hope, and buys the time to complete the large infrastructure programs."

Kirk pointed out that in the summer of 2003 we had put sixteen thousand people to work in Sadr City and moved around freely, collecting friendly high fives from the residents. Unfortunately, the CPA had failed to see the value of cleaning up trash and ordered us to end the program. Now, we were waiting to go back into Sadr City, as soon as the 1st Cav could make it safe.

We went on to explain the doctrine of post-conflict transition. We said it also dictated the need to simultaneously work at the national level on economic policy reform, democratization, security, the rule of law, civil society, and private sector development.

The group listened politely, but their questions demonstrated they were less interested in our views on reconstruction than in our ability to deliver large numbers of temporary jobs almost anywhere in the country. (At that time, an uneasy truce existed between the Iraqi Interim Government and Moktada al-Sadr, but Fallujah, Najaf, Karbala, Ramadi, Samarra, and Tal Afar were essentially in the hands of insurgents.) Stratman opined that we needed a way to pry young men away from the insurgency, and temporary employment seemed to work. As Pete Chiarelli had said, "Get them to put down the AK-47 and wrap their hands around a D-handle shovel." I pointed out that not only was Major General Chiarelli correct but that he also understood the temporary job was exactly that—temporary. While providing temporary employment, we also had to establish the enabling environment for economic growth and sustainable jobs. (Chiarelli understood the need for long-term development to restore the economy. He even transferred $2 million to USAID so we could provide grants and loans to Iraqi entrepreneurs in Baghdad.)

Hank Stratman understood perfectly but was not impressed with my primer on post-conflict transition. I said, "Look, Hank, I believe in what OTI can do. Kirk turned his entire operation on a dime to meet Pete Chiarelli's needs. I know it is working. But what happens when the money runs out and there are no permanent jobs? Take away the shovel, and that guy is going to pick up the AK-47 he has in the closet."

Stratman replied, "Spike, my goal is to reduce the violence enough to get us past the January elections. I understand what you are saying, but until then I am buying force protection."

I was stunned and said, "But Hank, what does that really buy us?"

The OGA operative replied, "A Shia government."

"Then you will have a civil war," I replied.

The OGA operative shrugged, as if it was inevitable.

Hank asked me how many people we could put to work on a daily basis. I turned to Kirk, who hesitated for several seconds and said, "Forty thousand, but we will run out of money by October, unless we get more from the realignment."

As we were leaving, I asked Kirk if he could really deliver that many jobs a day.

He said, "I guess we'll have to."

Kirk Day was a laconic, thirty-something redhead whose hair was too long. He was usually unshaven and often looked as if he had been wearing his baggy jeans for days. He was blunt but so soft-spoken I often had to ask him to repeat himself. He had cut his teeth in the Congo, East Timor, and Kosovo and was as tough as nails. He drove his young staff and contractors hard, but they loved him. When Pete Chiarelli had first laid out his plan, Kirk immediately understood he was talking about a strategic change in direction that required bold changes to what OTI had been doing. He turned OTI into an employment machine, and he did it in a matter of days. Not long after our partnership with the 1st Cav began, Pete Chiarelli invited Kirk, Bechtel representatives, and me to his Camp Victory headquarters, where he briefed Deputy Defense Secretary Paul Wolfowitz and several visiting generals. In a large conference room, packed with perhaps a hundred military and civilian officials, Chiarelli introduced everyone at the table. When he came to Kirk, slouched in his chair and looking about as unmilitary as one can look, Chiarelli said "And that young man, sir—Kirk Day—is a goddamned hero." It was the only time I ever saw Kirk blush.

In July, the first cease-fire with Moktada al-Sadr did allow us to get back into Sadr City. Chiarelli and his staff had plotted the most deprived areas and made a plan to immediate employ thousands of young men to clean up battle damage and solid waste, drain pools of standing sewage, and dig trenches for water and sewage pipes. OTI delivered on the jobs, and both Iraqis and the 1st Cav realized immediate benefits. The 1st Cav, which had been locked in combat with Moktada al-Sadr's Mahdi Army only weeks earlier, interacted with community leaders and undertook an information blitz to inform the population and win its cooperation. We were making significant headway.

But the Coalition and the Iraqi Interim Government lost patience with the Mahdi Army's occupation of Najaf and Karbala and in early

August launched a combined operation to take back both cities. Heavy fighting in Najaf and the Mahdi Army's losses caused the fighting to spill over into Sadr City. It also appeared to the 1st Cav that the massive investments in Sadr City were diminishing the influence of the Sadrists, who used the fighting in Najaf as an excuse to break the truce in Sadr City. The 1st Cav and the Mahdi Army were again locked in street fighting. This time, however, the Mahdi Army enjoyed only a modicum of support from the population and took heavy casualties. By September, we were back in Sadr City and renewed our efforts. With massive targeted assistance and a grudging cease-fire from a badly mauled Moktada al-Sadr, Sadr City would become for the next year the safest and least violent district of Baghdad.

In August, I was slated to return to Washington for consultations. Just before I left, Jadranka Spasojevic, who had been my secretary in Belgrade, arrived in Baghdad for a six-month voluntary assignment. She was a welcome addition to the palace office and the mission. As she had not yet been assigned permanent housing and was being moved from house to house, I offered her my house for the several weeks I would be away. My assigned house was one of three that faced the OTI office, across an open expanse of concrete tile we called the "piazza." We had to navigate the piazza's open space to get from the rest of the housing to the office trailers. One night while I was in Washington, Jadranka, Teddy Bryan, Mike Jones, and Chris Milligan were talking in front of my house when a 107-mm rocket came buzzing overhead. (The Chinese-made 107-mm rocket was a finless model that was crudely aimed and made a buzzing sound. Many were from old stocks of ordnance and, thankfully, did not explode, but rarely would all the rockets in a salvo fail to explode.) The entire group dropped all their gear and bolted through the door of my quarters. When another rocket buzzed overhead, they crawled into my bathroom, which offered greater safety. In all, they heard six rockets go over, but none of them exploded. Chris joked that they had not exploded because they were a new kind of smart rocket that actually came to the door and knocked—then exploded.

At that moment there was a loud knock on the door, which made everyone jump. It was not a smart rocket but a member of our Marine security detachment who had seen the radios, backpacks, and other gear the group had dropped on my porch. The corporal was just checking to see if everyone was all right. By this time, they had been on the bathroom floor for over an hour. They crawled into the living room and turned on the television to watch the Olympics. Jadranka, whose nerves were considerably frayed, asked if anyone knew where I kept my Scotch. They reported that there was only enough for one drink apiece, and nothing was in the larder when I returned. The incident became one of those gallows humor tales they told again and again.

I returned to Iraq at the end of August with guarded optimism. In security terms, it had been a rough spring and summer. April had been a disaster, followed by a lull from mid-May to mid-June. In June four of our expatriate contractors and even more of their Iraqi employees were killed. Our Iraqi building contractor working on the compound had repeatedly been targeted but stayed on the job, despite the killings. Conditions had improved in Sadr City in July, but August saw heavy fighting both there and in Najaf.

On June 28 I had given an interview to Knight-Ridder in which I said, "Security trumps everything. It does us little good to build a school if parents are afraid to send their children to that school because they may not come home." My words were widely quoted.

We kept hoping we would reach a tipping point where our reconstruction efforts would win over enough Iraqis that the insurgents would gradually lose popular support. Unfortunately, the insurgents had a vote, and they were banking on chaos and fear to stymie any effort at physical, social, or political reconstruction. Still, in Ambassador Negroponte we had a leader, and the realignment of funding offered hope that we were putting the program on the right track. The new Iraqi government's prime minister, Ayad Allawi, appeared to be a leader, too. My part of the program was greatly expanded, and we focused on the areas we thought offered Iraq its best chance. I had the right staff, and Ambassador Bill Taylor's scheduled arrival in September to take over IRMO presaged a new spirit of cooperation and sense of direction. Security would trump everything. But Negroponte

put it best, when responding to a query as to whether we were winning the war: "This is hard business, and the outcome is still in doubt."

Early in the morning on September 12—still September 11 in
the United States—Sunni insurgents launched a bold attack against
1st Cav troops that were patrolling just outside the Green Zone. In
our compound, we awoke at three o'clock to the sound of incoming
rockets and the deafening roar of a firefight in the area of the Assassin's
Gate, only a few hundred meters away. Small arms rounds were landing in the compound, and we could not tell if rockets were impacting
in the compound or next to it. Everyone was locked down, and many
spent hours on their bathroom floors. We had no casualties, but we
had no idea what was happening. I could clearly hear the clatter of
AK-47s and the louder return fire of the Bradley fighting vehicles'
25-mm chain guns. It sounded as if the insurgents, as long feared,
had breached the Green Zone and were in our sector. Later, we
would learn from CNN the fighting had been on Haifa Street, just
outside the Assassin's Gate, and a Bradley fighting vehicle had
been crippled and abandoned. The 1st Cav had been forced to pull
back and had called in an AH-64 Apache helicopter to destroy the
Bradley. The report said when the vehicle was destroyed, jubilant
Iraqis were swarming it. More than a dozen, including an Iraqi reporter, were killed.

A few nights later, I was watching a movie with Teddy at her
place, when the sound of an incoming rocket sent us to the floor. As
we hit the floor, Teddy shouted, "That hit right behind my kitchen! It
didn't explode, but I heard dirt and stones hit the side of the house."

I was not nearly so observant, but I realized I was bleeding from
the chest. When I told Teddy, she said, "But nothing came through
the walls or windows."

"I know," I replied, "but I'm still bleeding."

As it happened, Teddy's panicked cat had launched himself off
my chest with his hind claws when the rocket hit.

We immediately advised our security attachment that we thought
an unexploded rocket was directly behind Teddy's house. A few minutes later a Marine officer knocked on the door and confirmed a small
crater was directly behind the house. All the houses around it would

have to be evacuated. The rocket had not exploded, but it had buried itself two meters into the ground. An ordnance disposal unit would have to remove it. In the end, they had to blow it up in place, and at about three o'clock in the morning, they woke everyone, warning, "Fire in the hole!" The explosion rained shrapnel and clods of dirt all over the compound.

My Diplomatic Security friends Rick Lubow and Benito Bennett were so amused by the story and my wound they presented me with the "Purple Eggplant Award." (I still have it.)

On September 22, accompanied by several Bechtel employees, Teddy Bryan, Rick Whitaker, and I boarded two Black Hawk helicopters and flew to Saddam Hussein's tribal home of Tikrit. Bechtel had been working for over a year to reconstruct the Tikrit Bridge, which connected the cities of Kirkuk and Tikrit and had been destroyed in March 2003 by a Coalition air strike. Bob Davidson, our regional coordinator for northern Iraq, convoyed down from Irbil. The bridge was due to be completed in April 2004, but insurgents had repeatedly targeted the construction crews. A busload of Iraqi workers traveling from Kirkuk to Tikrit had been ambushed and slaughtered, but the Iraqi contractor and Bechtel had stayed on the job. Completion was late, but the bridge was now ready to be inaugurated.

We were met by Col. Randall Dragon of the 1st Infantry Division, which had barricaded both ends of the bridge. Hamad Hamood Shekti, the provincial governor, perhaps seventy-five local dignitaries, and members of the Western press who had accompanied our group also joined us. The surface of the bridge was still tacky because the asphalt had been laid down the day before and was melting in the heat. It stuck to our shoes, freezing the guests in their tracks. Teddy, weighed down by body armor, literally stuck to the bridge and had to be rescued. The 1st Division's marching band, replete with M-16 rifles draped over their shoulders, played Sousa. Colonel Dragon, the governor, and I made short speeches, as AH-64 Apache gunships and OH-58 Kiowa scout helicopters patrolled overhead. In Baghdad, meanwhile, British engineering consultant Kenneth Bigley pled unsuccessfully on Al Jazeera for his life. That same day, two car bombs killed twenty-one Iraqis. Unaware, we returned to the 1st Division headquarters for lunch and then flew back to the Green Zone.

My birthday was on September 24, and a small group of colleagues surprised me with a party. They enlisted the help of an Iraqi employee to purchase a cake, decorated with a birthday message. Somewhere in the translation from English to Arabic and back to English, the message on the cake ended up reading, "Happy Bathday Spic." It was the nicest cake I ever received.

We at USAID experienced a continuing battle over data concerning our projects. Before my arrival, USAID had contracted for a monitoring and evaluation system. I felt the product was inadequate and did not exercise the option for the contract's second phase. Our Washington offices solicited bids for a new contract to remodel an off-the-shelf system for our use. In the meantime, we struggled along with the inadequate system we had, inputting data manually. PCO contracted for its own data management system, but it too ran into problems.

With the arrival of General Casey, we were suddenly swamped with requests for data we did not collect and in formats we did not use. We did our best to provide what we could, but we were reluctant to provide raw data—particularly coordinates of projects—lest it be misconstrued or endanger our contractors or beneficiaries. After one occasion when I declined to respond to a blanket request for data, we received a visit from a U.S. Army lieutenant colonel and a New Zealand Army colonel from General Stratman's PME section. After introductions, they asked for direct access to our data system. I explained access to the data system was restricted, and in any case we did not want Multi-National Forces Iraq to extract raw data that could be misconstrued or even endanger our partners. The lieutenant colonel responded he actually already had access to our database and was intimately familiar with all our operations. If I would not authorize access, he said he would get the data anyway.

I was furious at his arrogance and the violation of our system. It was the closest I came to throwing someone out of my office and the only unpleasant encounter I had with anyone in the military during my tour. I informed him we would change every password to the system, and if he required anything further of me, he should ask Hank Stratman to speak with me directly. At the next country team meeting, Hank rather ruefully apologized for the encounter, and I explained our position. Eventually, IRMO set up an information fusion cell that received requests for information and disseminated reports. This cell ameliorated the problem, but MNFI was so large and the demand for data throughout its divisions was so great that it never really went away.

It was unusual for us at USAID to inaugurate any of our nine thousand projects. By March 2004, we determined publicity about our accomplishments put our contractors, the Iraqi beneficiaries, and the facilities themselves at risk. We had a daily report that went out by electronic mail to hundreds of subscribers, and we had a website. By April, I had ordered that our publications could not show any Iraqi faces, and facilities were to be described in only the most general terms. I took tremendous criticism from Washington, particularly from USAID's Bureau for Legislative and Public Affairs (LPA), even though under the CPA, General Oster had also ordered circumspection in publicity that could be used by the insurgents. Unfortunately, enforcement of the order was erratic. It was admittedly a conundrum. The Coalition could not win the Iraqis' hearts and minds if they were not informed that we were delivering real assistance, but public information could and did lead to murders and the destruction of completed facilities. The LPA continued to vilify my orders, even after the events of September 30 proved me right.

Our partnership with the 1st Cav had achieved significant results in Baghdad, in spite of the August and September fighting in Sadr City. The Project Contracting Office had been brought into the partnership, and its U.S. contractors were also completing projects. My arrangement with Major General Chiarelli and his staff was that the 1st Cav would not announce the completion of projects without my specific permission, but that did not necessarily apply to PCO contractors. On September 30, the 1st Cav held a ribbon-cutting ceremony to mark the completion of a pumping station in the poor Baghdad neighborhood of Hay al-Amal. Soldiers were handing out candy to children when the first of three car bombs exploded. The second and third detonated when rescue workers tried to aid the victims. Forty-one Iraqis—thirty of them children—were killed, and scores were wounded. Abu Musab al-Zarqawi claimed responsibility. October would be worse.

14  PARTNERS

Much has been made in the press about the U.S. government's use of unscrupulous, money-grubbing contractors to do reconstruction work in Iraq and to provide logistical support to the military. To many, Halliburton and its subsidiary Kellogg, Brown and Root (KBR) became synonymous with greed, poor delivery, and corrupt contracting by government officials. People tend to lump all providers of services in Iraq into a single group of bad actors. I do not subscribe to that view.

Since the 1970s, USAID has relied on "partners," that term being defined as grantees and contractors. Grantees are nongovernment, nonprofit organizations and are universally referred to as NGOs. They range from such groups as the International Committee of the Red Cross (ICRC) and CARE to those that deliver specialized technical assistance, such as microcredit and community development programs. Others assist in democratic development, civil society, and elections. Strict federal assistance and acquisition regulations ensure all grants are openly competed, with all applicants given a fair chance to win the award of grants. Grantees are subject to U.S. government audit and strict regulations regarding financial and operational records. Audits include assessments of both performance and financial accountability.

Contracts may be used for the same services that NGOs sometimes provide but are usually employed to obtain services from for-profit companies that provide specialized assistance, such as economic policy reform and restructuring, architectural and engineering work, construction management, and health and education programs. Again, the Federal Acquisition Regulations (FAR) provide strict controls for the acquisition process and the administration of all contracts. They require annual audits by reputable accounting firms and frequent U.S. government–administered performance and financial audits. Although there are several different types of contracts, there are specific guidelines for the amount of profit a contractor can earn. Warranted U.S. government contracting officers determine all contracts and grants and assist trained technical officers in contract or grant administration once an award is made. In USAID, we had highly competent contracting officers in Baghdad, in our satellite office in Jordan, and in Washington.

By law, NGO grantees receive less oversight than contractors, though in my experience they receive almost as much as contractors. For every instrument—contract or grant—a U.S. government cognizant technical officer (CTO) has a statutory responsibility to oversee the project. No CTO and no partner wants to be the subject of a critical audit with a finding of wrongdoing and poor oversight, so they tend to work together and support each other in the product's delivery. In Iraq, USAID placed a regional inspector general, six auditors, and a criminal investigator in the Green Zone. They shared our offices and residences, attended my senior staff meetings, and interacted daily with my staff. "Concurrent audits" helped our partners and us avoid mistakes. By the end of my tour, the auditors and the Defense Contracting and Audit Agency (DCAA) had completed approximately fifty audits, financial assessments, and several investigations. They found few instances of poor performance and one case where they suspected ancillary illegal activity, but most findings involved costs that were disallowed, a common finding anywhere. The costs either are justified after submitting additional documentation or are repaid to the U.S. Treasury. No one enjoys an audit, but they are an accepted and routine part of program implementation.

Much press was made of several large USAID contracts awarded under limited competition at the beginning of our involvement with Iraq. Under the Federal Acquisition Regulations, the award of a contract, from solicitation to award, normally takes four to eight months.

The regulations themselves provide for circumstances that justify sole-source procurements and limited-competition awards. The special inspector general for Iraq completely exonerated USAID of any wrongdoing regarding its limited-competition awards and praised it for placing the USAID inspector general on the ground in Iraq from the beginning.

Much criticism has also been leveled at the reconstruction program's employment of private security details. Most PSDs came from reputable companies that had strict hiring standards and enforced reasonable rules of engagement for their operations. This was certainly our experience with Kroll, a British company that provides security services worldwide. The men who protected us were veterans of the British Special Air Service, paratroopers, Royal Marines, and Gurkhas. They were highly trained, calm, and professional. I never witnessed or received reports of any abuse by Kroll of Iraqi citizens or their property. Their duties were extraordinarily dangerous. We were high-value targets, and they risked their lives every day they escorted us into the Red Zone.

USAID and our partners, who included hundreds of Iraqi subcontractors and thousands of Iraqi employees, operated in all eighteen governorates of Iraq. Often, we had people working in such hot spots as Fallujah, Baquba, and Samarra without the knowledge of the insurgents or the military. It was the only way they could survive and accomplish their work. Others were threatened, kidnapped, driven out of towns, or even killed. Few were headquartered in the Green Zone, and those who were had both expatriate and Iraqi staff spread all over Iraq. During my tenure in Iraq, fifteen of those expatriates died, along with more than fifty Iraqis. By mid-2006, the death toll among all Coalition expatriate contractors was more than six hundred. The number of their Iraqi employees who have died is exponentially higher.

Our partners deserve to be honored for their service, not vilified. They merit an accounting of their ingenuity, perseverance, and courage, but that story will have to wait. Too many of them are still serving in Iraq. Singling them out for praise would put them at greater risk. Bechtel, with its $2.4 billion construction effort, was well known in Iraq, the subject of many articles, and has now completed its contract. I have written about it because reference to it no longer jeopardizes its employees.

15  ATTRITION

Ambassador William Taylor arrived in mid-September 2004 but could not assume leadership of the Iraq Reconstruction Management Office until Admiral Nash departed at the end of the month. In the meantime, Bill met with key staff members, attended Nash's meetings with senior advisers, and generally familiarized himself with the program. Also in September, the $3.46 billion realignment of the reconstruction program was announced: $2.28 billion was allotted to various programs to improve security and train Iraqi security forces while the water and electricity sectors were reduced by more than $3 billion. USAID received approximately $800 million in new funding to carry out more transformational assistance, support the Iraqi Interim Government, and help prepare for elections.

After Admiral Nash's departure, I learned he had left a parting surprise. In the fourth quarter we received from the Office of Management and Budget some of the new funds that the realignment had awarded to us. We had also requested funding for Bechtel construction task orders that had been awarded to us from IRMO; however, before IRMO submitted the 2207 report to OMB, IRMO had deleted or pushed into the next fiscal year all construction requests except those for the Project Contracting Office. At the time, Admiral Nash was the head of IRMO and PCO, which received $1.2 billion. Neither USAID nor the Army Corps of Engineers, the other two major construction-executing agencies, received anything. Nash could claim that in his judgment, priority lay entirely with PCO projects, but the allocation reeked of bias and favoritism. At this point, Bechtel had been mobilized for nine months, expecting $1.8 billion in construction task orders. It was now clear, with only about $800 million in task orders issued, the Bechtel contract would not be filled. I had no choice but to order Bechtel to begin demobilizing personnel who could no longer be justified.

Once Bill Taylor took charge of IRMO, one of his first tasks was to sit down with Charlie Hess, the new PCO director, and me. We all agreed that we wanted an end to the bad blood, that we were one team, and that IRMO would issue the work to the executing agency that could best perform the task. We also decided to meet in my office immediately after each country team meeting to improve program management and to resolve any problems before they could fester. Bill, Charlie, and I were in strong agreement, and I saw an immediate sea change in the entire program's management. We still encountered some holdover "hardheads," as Charlie called them, but relationships improved dramatically.

Bill also initiated weekly progress meetings that, though time-consuming and not particularly popular with either Charlie or me, were transparent and demonstrated the strengths and weaknesses of all executing agencies. They gave my staff a chance to report not just on construction but on the entire USAID program, which educated everyone about its enormous scope. Bill was critical but fair, and he would not tolerate petty squabbling and backbiting. He had confided in me that prior to Admiral Nash's departure, he had sat in on meetings with senior advisers and in PCO and had been appalled at how Nash had at best tolerated the bashing of USAID and its staff and at worst had encouraged it. Bill resolved such behavior would not be allowed on his watch. We finally started to pull together as one team.

Outside the Green Zone, after two months of fighting, the Mahdi Army had been mauled in Sadr City and Najaf, and Coalition forces began a push to pacify the worst-conflicted areas ahead of the parliamentary elections scheduled after the New Year. The violence escalated:

October 1: U.S. forces killed a hundred insurgents in
     Samarra. At the same time, we were already working in

Najaf, following heavy fighting with the Mahdi Army.

October 4: Twenty-one Iraqi civilians were killed in suicide car bombings. Fallujah was still cordoned, and Marines engaged in sporadic fighting as they probed insurgent defenses. Vehicle-borne suicide bombers, in addition to the normal roadside bombs, mortars, and small arms fire, constantly targeted the BIAP road. That night, a rocket hit directly behind my house, biting large chunks of concrete out of the T-walls Fernando Cossich's group had installed two days earlier. The only casualties were Chris Milligan's SUV, a forklift, and a roosting dove that was knocked out of a tree and promptly pounced upon by a cat. Iraqi cats were tough.

October 6: Intelligence on threats against the BIAP road forced us to cancel all convoys to the airport. The trips resumed the next day, but we held our breath until a large group reached the airport. Ironically, that same day, the Iraq Survey Group (ISG) announced that after fifteen months of searching, it discovered no evidence that Saddam Hussein possessed weapons of mass destruction before the war.

October 7: Moktada al-Sadr offered to disarm his militia in Sadr City as part of a Coalition peace initiative.

October 8: Kenneth Bigley's family confirmed he had been murdered. (Two Americans captured with him had been beheaded earlier.)

October 14: Suicide bombers detonated devices at the Green Zone Café and the open-air bazaar just down the street. The café was within walking distance of our compound, and we had only days earlier put all restaurants in the Green Zone off-limits because of our concerns that they were tempting targets. Improvised explosive devices had repeatedly been found within the Green Zone, with one discovered in front of the café only days earlier. Five died and eighteen were wounded. Chris Milligan, returning from the Steel Dragons' dining facility, had to navigate around the smoking debris and body parts in the road.

October 15: Another car bomb targeted a Baghdad police patrol, killing ten.

October 18: Thirteen more people died after suicide car bombings in Baghdad and Mosul.

October 19: Margaret Hassan, the Irish-born director of CARE in Iraq and a thirty-year resident of Baghdad, was kidnapped. A few days later, she appeared in a video, pleading for her life. Though her body was never recovered, authorities presumed she was murdered. She was well known to our humanitarian relief team. CARE subsequently withdrew from Iraq.

After the bombing of the Green Zone Café, we saw a flurry of security construction and newly established checkpoints. Nearly all facilities were enclosed with T-walls, turning what had been broad avenues into virtual tunnels. The drive from our compound to the palace, which previously had no checkpoints, now had at least two that were manned by military police (MPs). To gain entry to the palace by vehicle, drivers had to submit to full vehicle searches at two additional checkpoints, and Gurkha guards finally controlled the parking lots's entrances outside the palace.

Getting into the Green Zone became increasingly difficult for our Iraqi employees, who were often turned away at one gate and forced to try again at another. Standing in long lines, they were vulnerable to insurgent surveillance and targeting by suicide bombers. Several barely escaped suicide bomb attacks at the zone's various gates, and many received death threats at their homes. Ever resourceful, Fernando Cossich hired two expatriates to meet them at the gates and drive them to the compound. When employees were threatened in their homes, we gave them administrative leave to relocate. In some cases, we housed Iraqi employees in our compound until they could make other arrangements. When the KBR dining facilities started denying entry to Iraqi employees, Fernando had meals brought in from outside the Green Zone until our cafeteria was ready. Fernando took care of everyone, but he had a special place in his heart for the Iraqis. They returned his goodwill and humanity with great loyalty.

In November, I was asked to give an on-camera interview to Kimberly Dozier of CBS. She wanted to interview me in the palace office and to focus on the USAID efforts at reconstruction. Though I did give interviews, I was always leery of them and had been particularly cautious about giving them prior to the 2004 U.S. presidential elections. Dozier, however, had long experience in Iraq. I had seen her work on television, and I thought she was objective. With the elections over, I agreed to the interview. With her sound and cameramen, Dozier set up one morning in the palace office. The interview lasted about twenty minutes, and there were no surprises. She was particularly interested in the difficulty of doing reconstruction in the middle of a shooting war. I answered that it was difficult but doable and was at pains to talk about the thousands of projects we had completed that were not large construction efforts.

Dozier and her crew asked to see one of our projects and to shoot footage that would be aired with the interview. When they asked if they could visit Baghdad South, a large electricity generating plant being constructed by Bechtel, we agreed but with conditions. They could not mention its location or film any panoramic shots that could pinpoint the location, and they could not show any Iraqi workers' faces on camera. Dozier and her crew rode to the site in a Kroll-escorted convoy. As the convoy sped through Baghdad, Dozier interviewed Rick Whitaker and John Kretchmer of our infrastructure office. Rick and John, in body armor, talked about the risks of site visits. (The GE team members had been on its way to Baghdad South, back in June, when a suicide car bomber killed five of them.) The camera panned from the armed bodyguards to the view through the windshield as the cars wove through traffic. At the site, Dozier followed the rules, but the coverage of the site was still impressive.

When the story aired on CBS, the interview with me had been cut to a few sound bites. Most of the piece focused on the dangers of getting to the project sites and the risks taken by middle-aged civilians doing their jobs in a war zone. All of the footage was compelling and complimentary of our efforts, but it was not exactly the story we had agreed to do. I did not blame Kimberly Dozier. That is just the way the news business works. A reporter and her editors go with the best story.

Along with CNN, Kimberly Dozier interviewed me again just before my departure in March 2005. Both interviewers wanted my perspective after serving thirteen months in Iraq. To my knowledge, neither interview aired. In May 2006, Kimberly Dozier was severely wounded by a suicide bomber while filming U.S. troops on the streets of Baghdad. An American officer, an Iraqi translator, and both members of her crew were killed.

I have often been asked what emotions I experienced when taking a trip into the Red Zone. People want to know what it is like to strap on body armor and climb into an armored Suburban, knowing that it can be blown apart at any minute by a rocket-propelled grenade, an IED, or a vehicle-borne suicide bomber. The answer is not illuminating. We had an expression in Vietnam: "There it is." It meant we dealt with the reality we could die in a hundred ways and what could go wrong would go wrong. There was no personal choice in any of it—you had a job to do and you did it, hoping you would get out alive. In Iraq, the troops said, "Embrace the suck." They meant it all "sucked," and they got through their tours by flowing with it. I never wrote to my family before I went into the Red Zone, and I do not believe I wrote to them when I safely returned, either. I just simply dealt with it. When I was out in the Red Zone, though, my head was on a swivel. Unarmed, I prayed I could get to one of the weapons my PSD carried if I had to leave the vehicle. While we passengers all prayed not to be maimed, we prayed most often not to be captured and end up in an Al Jazeera video dressed in an orange jumpsuit. Death by gunshot, IED, or suicide bomber was comparatively better. We sent three car convoys into the Red Zone almost every day and sweated their safe return. We just embraced the suck.

In Washington, responsibility for hosting the weekly secure video teleconference had shifted from DOD to the State Department, but Frank Miller at the NSC really ran them. In Baghdad, Bill Taylor used the weekly progress meetings to shape the agenda for the SVTC and to move it along at a brisk pace. The NSC's major interests were electricity generation and employment. Weekly PowerPoint presentations were prepared, showing the number of jobs created by each executing agency and tracking the number of available megawatts of electricity. As USAID was responsible for producing at least forty thousand short-term jobs on any given day, we were always under pressure. Any drop in employment was scrutinized, and we had to defend it. USAID also had a half-dozen electricity generation projects, including several high-visibility ventures, under way. Most were behind schedule, as was almost every electricity generation project in Iraq, but two of ours were new plants that promised significant output of more than 500 megawatts. I was often on the hot seat at the SVTC, though I was not the only one.

One of our new generation plants was a gas-fired facility near Kirkuk. We had already installed a Siemens V64 generator at the plant and planned to install a far larger and more powerful Siemens V94. Together they would produce 325 megawatts. The V94 had been shipped to the port of Tartus on Syria's coast. With its carrier, the V94 weighed 400,000 pounds and moved seven kilometers per hour. In early summer, it had reached the Teshrin Dam near the Iraq border, when U.S. relations with Syria soured and the United States levied sanctions against Syria. Syrian authorities suddenly halted the V94 at the dam. After weeks of delays and the Syrian government's broken promises, Bechtel and I made the decision to turn the V94 around for a month-long journey across Syria to the Jordanian border, where it arrived safely. Unfortunately, its drivers then had to negotiate a much longer and more dangerous route across Iraq, straight through the heart of the Sunni insurgency. It required a military escort, and the military did not want to move it until Fallujah had been secured.

At the same time, we had two GE generators, each 108 megawatts, sitting in Jordan until the site at Baghdad South was ready for them. We did not want to ship them until they could be lifted directly onto the bolts of the large pads that Bechtel was constructing.

Frank Miller at the NSC relentlessly barraged me with questions as to why the three generators had not been moved into Iraq.

Why could they not be moved by air? We had already investigated that solution for transporting the V94. It was too large for a Russian Antonov 22, the largest aircraft in the world, and the Kirkuk air base could not accommodate an Antonov 22. Could it not be broken down into several pieces? It could, but that kind of operation should not be done in the field. Even if it were, it would take months to put it back together. Why were we planning to move it from Jordan into Iraq on Route 10? Route 10 was the only road from Jordan into Iraq. When would it move? The time frame depended on the military. Why could we not move the GE generators for Baghdad South? They were safe in Jordan, and we did not want to move them until the pads were ready.

We eventually moved the first of the 108-megawatt GE generators to Baghdad South and mounted it in place without incident. We soon moved the other, with the same result. Pressure increased to move the V94 to Kirkuk.

The Bechtel team, concerned about moving the V94 through the Ramadi-Fallujah area, continued searching for a route that would skirt both. In the Arabic notes of an Iraqi engineer who had died during the initial route surveys, a team member found a description (in Arabic) of a dirt road that had been built years earlier for oil exploration. According to the engineer's notes, the road ran far to the north and west of Ramadi and Fallujah, but it did not appear on any map and needed to be surveyed. A team drove in from Jordan but was attacked while trying to inspect the road. Still, it looked promising, and more survey attempts were made by helicopter. Bridges over the Euphrates and Tigris would have to be reinforced, and the shoring would have to be fabricated in Iraq and installed at the last possible moment, lest the work draw the insurgents' attention. A military escort—tanks, mechanized infantry, and helicopters—would have to be synchronized. We were ready, but the military was not.

Frank Miller continued to hammer away at me. Bill Taylor helped us in every way he could, but I was under a lot of pressure. We received a call from Sarah Lenti, an aide to National Security Adviser Condoleezza Rice. Ms. Lenti wanted a status report every other day on each of the USAID electricity generation projects, including daily movements (or not) of the V94. She also wanted a weekly telephone call. We were told that Dr. Rice required briefings every other day. I thought it overkill, but we did it. It was just one more example of what we referred to as the "eight-thousand-mile screwdriver."

The military would not move the V94 until the situation in Fallujah was resolved. After the ambush and mutilation of the Blackwater personnel in March, Ambassador Bremer and General Sanchez had ordered the Marine Expeditionary Force (MEF) to clean out Fallujah and then, in mid-assault, ordered them to pull back. There followed weeks of negotiation with Iraqi officials and tribal leaders. Much of the negotiation was handled by Ambassador Dick Jones, Bremer's deputy and an experienced, Arabic-speaking career diplomat for whom I had worked in Lebanon. Desperate for a solution, the Coalition agreed to the formation of the Fallujah Brigade, consisting of ex–Iraqi Army soldiers and led by ex–Iraqi Army officers, who were all Sunnis from the area. The Fallujah Brigade, rife with the very men who had perpetrated the Fallujah insurgency, was a disaster that resulted in the loss of all the weapons and other equipment it had received.

Over the summer, Sunni insurgents and foreign fighters consolidated their grip on Fallujah, subjecting the inhabitants to Sharia law and beating or executing anyone who objected. Air strikes and artillery assaults on suspected insurgent strongholds seemed to only further the insurgent's resolve and inflame the Arab "street" throughout the Middle East. Fallujah was an embarrassment—a beacon of American vulnerability—and it emboldened the insurgency in other cities in the Sunni Triangle. As summer turned to fall, we knew that the battle for Fallujah was coming, but we suspected it would not happen until after the U.S. presidential elections in November. In the meantime, the Marines tightened the cordon around the city and continued artillery and air strikes.

When the assault began in November, our only warning was a lockdown and what information we were able to glean from CNN and other cable networks. Once it was under way, we witnessed the airlift of medevacs, day and night, to and from the CSH. Incredibly, the USAID mission actually had Iraqi workers inside Fallujah until two days before the assault began, and they managed to safely extract themselves. We had also placed the Office of Transition Initiatives' Gail Long at Camp Fallujah to work with the incomparable Col. John Ballard, who led the Marines' civil affairs effort. They prepared for the effort to rebuild Fallujah once the insurgents had been killed, captured, or driven out.

In the end, Fallujah was nearly destroyed, but many insurgents escaped to raise havoc in such places as Mosul and Tal Afar. Mopping up and removing IEDs and unexploded ordnance would keep us out of Fallujah well into December, but the city would eventually become one of the safer places in Iraq, albeit rigidly controlled by the Marines. November was the bloodiest month for the Coalition, with more than 130 American soldiers killed in action.

The IIG announced that national parliamentary elections would be held January 30. The military, anticipating an increase in insurgent attacks leading up to the elections, postponed any movement of the V94 until after January 30.

Although some PCO projects began to "turn dirt" in October and November, pressure from DOD, the State Department, and the NSC to spend faster was relentless. U.S. "design-build" contractors were doing virtually all the construction work in Iraq. Large capital projects—electricity generation plants, water and sewer treatment, buildings, bridges—are not labor intensive and do not initially spend money very quickly. Washington erroneously observed that perhaps the program would move more quickly if it contracted directly with Iraqi firms. It made this assertion without any effort to determine if Iraqi firms had the capability. The truth of the matter was that design-build firms such as Bechtel employed hundreds of Iraqi subcontractors. Bechtel's experience, with eighteen months of doing business in Iraq, was that few Iraqi subcontractors could meet the requirements of the Federal Acquisition Regulations. Few had the cash flow to purchase materials, and they could not purchase insurance. Their construction standards did not meet requirements, they did not employ adequate safety standards, and they also could not comply with standard accounting practices. Bechtel had established what it called

"Bechtel U" to bring the best of the Iraqi contractors up to an acceptable standard to be used as subcontractors, but they were not at a level where we could contract directly with them.

If Bechtel, or any other of our partners, failed to perform or engaged in fraudulent practices, we had recourse through U.S. courts, even for the actions of their Iraqi subcontractors. Our partners bore the risk. If we were to contract directly with Iraqi contractors, however, recourse would be through weak Iraqi courts in which we would try to apply U.S. law.

Pressured to contract directly with Iraqi firms, I refused. I had a fiduciary responsibility to the American taxpayer, and I was not about to abrogate it. I also believed local contracting would neither result in any greater numbers of Iraqis being employed nor make the program move any faster.

In the meantime, together with the 1st Cav, we were pouring resources and effort into Sadr City in what rapidly became the most successful combination of combat and reconstruction. At the same time, we were working in Najaf with good results and making plans with the Marine Expeditionary Force (MEF) to go into Fallujah as soon as the situation on the ground would permit reconstruction. Shortly after major fighting in Fallujah ended, Bill Taylor visited the Marines and Camp Fallujah. Persuaded to drive to the mayor's headquarters within the city, his convoy came under fire. Sniping and ambushes slowed our efforts in Fallujah.

This was not the case in Sadr City. The 1st Cav had made Herculean efforts to remove unexploded ordnance and IEDs, and the population was cooperative. With new funding from the realignment, OTI was able to deliver on short-term employment in massive terms. Larger construction efforts, with a very heavy push from Major General Chiarelli, moved as quickly as possible. Sadr City settled down and stayed calm. The Mahdi Army and Moktada al-Sadr were still there, but, for the moment, they had decided reconstruction efforts were more in their interest than further fighting.

Pete Chiarelli told me the fighting in August and September had been very different from that of April through June. In the April battles, the insurgents had been numerous, seasoned, well trained, and mostly from Sadr City. They had enjoyed the people's protection and support. In August, they were fewer, younger, ill trained, and from farther south. Doors had not opened to them. The average citizen in Sadr City had been angered by the resumption of fighting. They wanted peace and the reconstruction benefits they had tasted in July. (Even in the highly critical book *Blood Money: Wasted Billions, Lost Lives, and Corporate Greed in Iraq* by T. Christian Miller (Little, Brown, 2006), Sadr City is seen as a model of how reconstruction should have been undertaken from the start.)

Unfortunately, squeezing the insurgents was similar to squeezing Jell-O: they would simply squirt out to threaten somewhere else. The cordon and assault of Fallujah had given rise to an enormous increase in fighting and killings in Mosul. In spite of our successes in Sadr City, Al Rashid, and Nine Nissan in eastern and southern Baghdad, fighting increased in Abu Ghraib and other areas of Baghdad as well as to the north in Baquba and Samarra. On November 24, the Green Zone was bombarded with more than sixty rockets and mortars. Four Gurkhas from Global Risk Strategies were killed and fifteen others wounded.

That same day, Jim Mollen was assassinated while driving alone in a Ministry of Education car in the Red Zone. Mollen was the senior adviser for education and had generally worked well with us. A holdover from the CPA who had been hired by IRMO, Jim was technically a State Department employee. I had seen him a few days before his death and was surprised he was still in Iraq. It was later reported that he had planned to be home for Thanksgiving. Driving himself in an unauthorized, thin-skinned vehicle around the Red Zone was an astounding violation of the rules. When such a death occurs, an Accountability Review Board (ARB) is required. Such boards can end an ambassador's career as well as those of others in the chain of responsibility. Condoleezza Rice did not order a board for the incident until February 28, 2005. The ARB's results were not sent to Congress until September 8, 2005. A Diplomatic Security Notice was issued November 21, 2005, mandating security directives from chiefs of missions to ensure all employees were informed and aware of the consequences for violating the directives, but that was the end of it.

The BIAP road was earning its reputation as the "road of death." In November, the embassy no longer permitted agencies' personnel and their private security details to send convoys to the airport. Instead, they would have to take armored buses called "Rhinos," which were escorted by heavily armed military convoys with air support, to and from the airport. Then, after one of the first convoys was hit by a suicide car bomber, the embassy decided to move the convoys only at night. This mandate wreaked havoc with the process of getting in and out of Iraq. Initially, Camp Stryker at BIAP had few facilities for passengers, who were often delayed there for two days waiting for a flight out or, upon returning, for a night convoy moving passengers to the Green Zone. Steve Browning was able to set up visitors' cots and blankets in the military tents at Camp Stryker, but with waits that could stretch to three days each way, getting in and out of Baghdad became a miserable proposition.

Iraqi nationals who worked for the embassy had to make their own way to and from the airport. We determined that we would offer Kroll-escorted travel to the airport for our Iraqi employees, who frequently traveled to Jordan and other points on official business. On December 6, a Kroll two-car armored convoy carrying two Iraqi employees to the airport was ambushed on the overpass just 500 meters from the Green Zone's Gate 12. A suicide bomber had darted between the two fully armored vehicles and detonated. The front end of the second FAV, carrying two Kroll bodyguards, was completely blown off. Miraculously, they suffered only flash burns and other minor injuries. They exited the burning car and were picked up by the badly damaged lead FAV, which returned to the Green Zone. That night, we visited the bodyguards at the Kroll House and brought them a case of beer. They were dazed, with their burns covered with ointment, but they were alive. Neither wanted to go home.

While our passengers and Kroll PSD were accounted for, we could not find the second FAV. This issue was a major problem because the vehicle contained radios and other sensitive equipment. Eventually, Fernando found it at BIAP, where the 1st Cav had deposited it. Although it was nothing but a burned-out shell, Fernando had it delivered to our junkyard at the back of the compound. FAVs cost as much as $250,000 each, and we cannibalized the wrecks for replacement parts. Keeping our vehicles maintained was a constant priority. Without them, we could not move, but even repairing bulletproof windshields, which cracked in Iraq's heat, had to be accomplished by DS-licensed technicians. Once, when we sent two vehicles to Jordan to be repaired, the truck carrying them was hijacked. Iraq was a nightmare of accountability for a civilian agency unaccustomed to operating in a war zone.

Everyone hated the Rhinos. Riders felt like targets in a tin can with little chance of getting out if hit by an IED, rocket-propelled grenade (RPG), or suicide bomber. Further, the embassy had a small number of Rhinos, so travelers backed up in the Green Zone and at the airport. On December 2, the Rhino convoys were abandoned, and an "air bridge" of Black Hawk helicopters began to make regular runs between the Green Zone and BIAP. This development was a vast improvement and unclogged the logjam. Everyone felt safer—we loved those Black Hawks—but from the military's standpoint the arrangement was not sustainable. The helicopters and their crews were needed elsewhere.

USAID administrator Andrew Natsios had not visited Iraq since November 2003 and wanted to come out prior to the Iraq elections. Although we welcomed his visit, not only had the logistics of getting in and out of Iraq become daunting, but we also expected the level of violence to ratchet up prior to the elections. Getting him out into the field and arranging meetings with Iraqi officials would be difficult. I tried to dissuade him, to no avail, and the visit was set for the second week of December. He was bringing with him a Fox News reporter and cameraman, a *Washington Times* reporter, Jeff Grieco from USAID's Legislative and Public Affairs, and an aide. Our planning took place during the November Fallujah assault, the bloodiest month in Iraq since April. We were still receiving rocket attacks, and the BIAP road was growing ever more dangerous. Air Serv picked up the party from Jordan, landed at Baghdad to refuel, and then flew them to our regional office in Irbil. In the Kurdish autonomous area, the group could move more freely to meet with officials and see some of our projects. I monitored the visit through reports from our coordinator, Bob Davidson. After several hours in Irbil, the party returned to Baghdad and was lifted by helicopter to the Green Zone, arriving at dusk.

We had arranged a dinner that night with Iraqi officials at the Al Rashid Hotel's restaurant. The hotel itself was then housing senior Iraqi officials and was off-limits to anyone without special identification. We had barely settled Andrew Natsios into his accommodations when I began to receive radio messages from Rebecca Bouchebel, our Lebanese public information officer. Grieco and the Fox News team had gone with her to the Al Rashid Hotel and were insisting on setting up an interview with Natsios in the lobby, which was off-limits. The MPs were threatening to arrest all of them and had confiscated Rebecca's ID card. Grieco was on the radio, broadcasting in the clear to one and all that he was in the Al Rashid Hotel preparing to interview the USAID administrator prior to his dinner there with Iraqi officials. I expected the rockets to start falling at any minute.

Grieco had never grasped the unique security situation in Iraq and had pilloried Chris Milligan and me for limiting coverage of our programs to protect lives and facilities. Now, after this incident, Chris and I talked to Andrew's aide and asked him to speak with Andrew about reining in Grieco. A few minutes later, I was in the armored car with Andrew. Though I talked by phone with Andrew every Friday, it was the first time we had met in months. Andrew had always been incredibly supportive of the mission and me personally, so I was surprised when he launched into a tirade about his need for press coverage to win his battles within the administration and averred that I just did not understand his position. Admitting that Grieco could be a problem and had stepped over the line, Andrew defended his intent and assailed my obstinacy in refusing to understand his problems in Washington. When pushed, I tend to push back. This time, however, I kept my mouth shut and just took it, embracing the suck. It was not an argument I could win, and I was facing two more days with the delegation.

The dinner came off without incident, though some Iraqi officials elected not to brave the trip to the Green Zone. By the time we rode back to the compound, Andrew had cooled off. Fox News wanted to conduct interviews and live broadcasts from the compound. We insisted that they not interview our Iraqi employees on camera unless their identities could be concealed, and we did not permit any filming of the compound. I was expecting another explosion from Andrew and Grieco, but thankfully it was avoided.

Pete Chiarelli had graciously agreed to provide us with helicopters, which we boarded the next morning and flew through wind and rain to the Bechtel camp at Taza near Kirkuk. It was bitterly cold in the Black Hawks, as the wind from the open hatches of the gunners coursed through the cabin. Taza was the site of a new gas-fired electricity-generating facility—the same one waiting for the V94. We arrived without incident and met the Bechtel team and the local mayor, who, surprisingly, agreed to be interviewed on camera. After a two-hour visit, we flew to Camp Fallujah. The Marines were still mopping up in Fallujah a few miles away. While Andrew and I met with the commanding general and his staff, the reporters disappeared. A base full of Marines who were still fighting in Fallujah was a smorgasbord for the press. By then, it was getting dark, and the weather steadily worsened. The pilots wanted to go, but we could not find the reporters and Grieco. Andrew and I boarded the helicopter and waited while our Marine hosts searched. Through the intercom, the pilot told me if the rest of the party did not show up in five minutes, they would be left behind. Just before the deadline, the Marines found and delivered them to the landing zone in a pickup truck, and we departed for the twenty-minute flight to LZ Washington.

That night, we hosted a dinner at the USAID cafeteria for the visitors and our staff. Deputy Chief of Mission Jim Jeffrey represented the ambassador. We had assembled senior staff members to brief Andrew prior to the dinner, while the remainder waited. Following the briefing, everyone sat down for a buffet dinner. The staff had been waiting for over an hour to eat and was getting restless. Unfortunately, speeches preceded dinner, and my troops were getting close to open rebellion. Finally, when Andrew asked if anyone had questions, I was able to interject that perhaps we should eat first. There was an audible sigh around the room and a rush for the buffet line. The dinner ended a long day.

The next morning, the delegation departed for BIAP and an Air Serv flight to our regional office in Basra. I sent several minders with them. Tom Staal handled the visit with aplomb, and the group saw some projects close to the base and took some good pictures. After several hours, Andrew and the delegation flew back to Jordan. We exhaled and got back to work.

Our Iraqi staff wanted a Christmas party. For weeks they decorated the cafeteria and deposited presents for the expatriate staff in front of a virtual Christmas tree that they had taped to the wall. For our part, we chipped in, and Fernando's crew bought presents for the children of our Iraqi employees. LPA sent a large box of presents as well from Washington. Fernando also arranged for a Christmas party in the cafeteria, where we laid out hundreds of presents on a bank of tables. Iraqi food was brought in, and we played canned music. It was a joyful occasion, with Iraqis breaking into traditional folk dancing and expatriates making fools of themselves trying to duplicate the complex steps. A talented Iraqi employee regaled us with hilarious impersonations of Chris and me, among others.

As the party began to break up, the same employee approached me and said the cleaning ladies wanted to speak to me. He offered to translate as most of them spoke only a few words of English and my Arabic was rudimentary. As he translated, I learned all of the cleaning ladies were Christians. Throughout December, Baghdad's churches had been subjected to bombings and arson. Church leaders had canceled all worship and celebrations of Christmas. The ladies wanted to thank me for the party and the gifts for their children. I learned it was the only Christmas celebration they would have. They were all in tears, and I had difficulty maintaining my composure.

On Christmas Day, we Americans and expatriates cooked dinner for the cafeteria staff and those Iraqis who were on twenty-four-hour duty. I left the dinner to deliver a plate to an ailing colleague. As I was crossing the drive, mortar rounds started hitting near the compound. With my hands full, I broke my own rules that I had drilled into everyone: lie flat and stay there. Instead, I crouched in the middle of the road until the barrage lifted. Looking at the tinfoil-covered plates, I thought, "You idiot, you could have died for turkey and sweet potatoes."

One consequence of the transition to an embassy was that the RSO wanted to bring USAID under the security umbrella of its contract with DynCorp. We were comfortable with Kroll and had worked out over a long period the procedures for static security at our Green Zone compound and at our three regional offices. Kroll was entirely professional and responsive to our needs, and we felt its employees were part of our extended family. Other security providers greatly varied in quality, particularly as the demand increased for their services. Kroll personnel were all former British paratroopers, Royal Marines, Special Air Service, or Gurkhas. We had experienced none of the problems others had with poorly trained, "cowboy" PSDs. For our static security, Kroll had provided fifty-six Gurkhas under the command of a former British officer who spoke Nepalese and ran a tight operation. Also, DynCorp would report to DS, and we feared we would lose control and quality of service.

My colleagues in Washington and I fought the change for months, but DS was adamant, even though DynCorp's services would cost $10 million more a year. We lost the battle, and DynCorp took over on December 31. We were only able to retain Kroll under separate contract to provide the intelligence fusion cell and continue to produce the daily security report. DynCorp proved competent PSDs, but we missed the comfort level we had achieved with Kroll.

In early January, on a bright sunny day, the Kroll Gurkhas conducted a formal changing of the guard with the Gurkhas whom DS provided from Global Risk Strategies. It was a full military ceremony with British pomp and flair. I thanked them for their service to us. Fernando and I were each presented with a khukri, the curved fighting knife every Gurkha carried. Others were presented with silver pins that depicted the khukri. We shook hands with each of them, and there were more than a few tears. We were all saddened by their departure, but we had no choice.

Our partners were not eligible to use the air bridge and still had to navigate the BIAP road. It weighed heavily on me and with good reason. On January 3, our contractor BearingPoint sent a convoy with two expatriate staff members to the airport. A suicide car bomber hit them at the same location we had been hit the month before. The armored car carrying the passengers was blown completely off the overpass. It fell to the street below, where it was consumed by fire. The two Kroll bodyguards and both passengers were killed. It was a hard blow for all of us and particularly for BearingPoint's team. The group had been with us from the beginning, and we knew all of the staff well. Tracy Hushin, BearingPoint's vivacious thirty-four-year-old operations manager, was one of the victims. She had gone to the airport to make travel arrangements for sixty Iraqi officials whom BearingPoint was sending overseas for training. The attack occurred on the return trip, when they were almost inside the relative safety of the Green Zone. BearingPoint swallowed hard but decided to remain in Iraq.

16

JUST A LITTLE LIGHT

While visiting my parents before my Iraq tour, I received a call from Teddy Bryan, who was attending leadership training at the prestigious Federal Executive Institute in Charlottesville, Virginia. At the time, I was actively recruiting USAID Foreign Service officers with post-conflict experience willing to join me in Iraq. In spite of USAID's system for bidding on positions, that is the way it is done: people hire those they know. At her leadership training, Teddy had been impressed with Jennifer Link, a democracy officer then assigned to Moscow. A lawyer with broad experience, particularly in Eastern Europe, Jennifer was interested in serving in Iraq. I needed a leader for USAID's democracy office, which oversaw substantial local governance and community development programs and was slated to receive more funding for its civil society project. In January 2004, decisions had not yet been made about the timing of parliamentary elections or how international donors would provide support, but I knew USAID would have a role.

Jennifer called me on my cell phone, and we talked for perhaps twenty minutes. I asked questions about her experience, and we both discussed our deep commitment to instilling democratic principles and building democratic structures in post-conflict countries. I liked "the cut of her jib" and asked about her relationships in Moscow. She was unmarried and felt she could leave her job in Moscow early with little bruising. I offered her the job of chief of the democracy office and told her I needed to know within forty-eight hours if she would accept, explaining that if she did, she would definitely go to Iraq and soon. She accepted immediately, and I went to work on the personnel system to get her to Baghdad as soon as possible.

Under the CPA, the Office of Democracy and Governance (ODG) was an island of competence in a sea of dysfunction. It had some experienced Foreign Service officers, such as Dean Pittman, whom I had known when he worked the Balkans at the NSC, and Judy Van Rest, who headed the office. Judy had broad experience in USAID, the Peace Corps, and the International Republican Institute, where she had led democracy efforts in Eastern Europe. Congress had mandated $100 million of the supplemental appropriations be used for democracy building, but Judy and Dean had persuaded Ambassador Bremer to more than triple that amount. In the spring of 2004, we worked with ODG to design projects in civil society, parliamentary support, support to the cabinet, and, most important, support for elections. As part of our strategy to position ourselves for the realignment once the State Department took over in July, we competed these efforts and awarded contracts, gambling that we would get the funding.

Election support consists of drafting laws to enable elections, supplying administrative support to conduct the elections, hiring and training election staff, training indigenous election monitors, educating the electorate, conducting information campaigns to encourage people to vote, facilitating international election observers, and supporting the fair and transparent conduct of the elections. It is the host country's responsibility to carry out the elections, but they are often conducted under the auspices of the United Nations or other international bodies. CPA Order Number 92 created the Independent Electoral Commission of Iraq in May 2004, and its membership included a UN elections expert. The director of the UN Electoral Assistance Division, Carina Perelli, visited Baghdad and appointed Carlos Valenzuela to sit on the commission. An experienced practitioner of organizing elections, Valenzuela was a good choice, but the UN had few resources in Iraq. We had already made grants totaling $87 million to IFES (formerly the International Federation for Electoral Support), an international NGO dedicated to building democratic societies; the International Republican Institute (IRI); and the National Democratic Institute (NDI). All had great expertise and experience in election support, and each brought particular strengths. In taking on the challenge, they all showed great courage, given the environment of violence in Iraq.

The Transitional Administrative Law, which took effect on June 28, 2004, mandated that parliamentary elections for a transitional government be held not later than January 31, 2005. Elections usually take as much as two years to organize properly. We had seven months.

Jennifer Link dived into the task of making the elections happen. We had agreed with Carlos Valenzuela and Carina Perelli that the UN should be the face of international support and that USAID and our team would support the UN as anonymously as possible. We did not want it to appear that the United States was running the elections, and we all agreed the Electoral Commission had to be put in the driver's seat. Jennifer masterfully managed our disparate actors and worked with Carlos. The elections' success soon became a consuming policy objective, and Jennifer proved just as masterful at dealing with the various interagency interlocutors who wanted to "help."

Some of the help offered was decidedly unwanted and dangerous. We were providing training to any of the four hundred political parties that wanted assistance. Obviously to us, we could not discriminate among parties, as such bias violated the democratic principles we were trying to instill and gave the appearance we were trying to influence the outcome. As January drew closer, however, some staffers in State and in the NSC argued for direct funding to selected political parties. We wanted no part of it and argued against it. In the end, nothing came of their efforts, to my knowledge, but for months they were distractions we did not need.

In November, after much press speculation that the violence in Iraq would force the postponement of elections, the Electoral Commission announced national elections would take place on January 30. We had always been working toward elections in January, but now the date was set. The pressure to succeed was intense. Just as intense was the insurgents' determination to foil the elections. Violence increased, and pundits surmised that holding fair elections in such an atmosphere was impossible. Sunni leaders urged their followers to boycott the elections.

Security for the elections fell on Coalition forces and the nascent Iraqi security forces. We also needed the military to distribute seven million pounds of ballots and voting equipment, in an atmosphere where the Electoral Commission could not announce the location of polling stations until the last minute. One glitch that threatened to upset everything was the need to identify each of the parties and have their logos printed on the ballots overseas. We had to have the material to the printer by a certain date, if the printer was to print them and get them to Iraq in time. It was a tight schedule.

Three weeks before the elections, Chris Milligan and I had a conversation with Jennifer. By this point I knew that even if everything else we did in the reconstruction were to be a complete success—which it wouldn't—failed elections would be our legacy. When I asked Jennifer if we were going to pull them off, she replied that to date we had hit every benchmark on the team's timeline; however, she could not guarantee the elections would take place. We also worried the Iraqis would not turn out in legitimate numbers or would be intimidated from voting. A real concern was that no one would show up at the polls. So many factors could doom the effort. All we could do then was make sure that we did our part, hope that others did their part, and pray. I asked for daily updates and crossed my fingers.

Every single day that January the insurgents inflicted some new horror on the Iraqi people and Coalition forces. Prime Minister Allawi, in spite of calls to postpone the elections, held firm and announced that they would go forward as planned. On January 26, the Coalition suffered its worst one-day losses in Iraq when thirty-seven soldiers were killed.

On January 28, Iraqi expatriates cast their ballots at polling places in Europe, the United States, and the Middle East. The turnout was higher than expected. Press coverage showed Iraqi expatriates who had traveled for days and dressed as if attending a wedding. They voted and expressed their joy. What we had thought would be a sideshow was a success. In Iraq, meanwhile, the government had closed the airports and imposed a broad three-day curfew for the elections, including a ban on all but official vehicles. Iraqis would have to walk to the polling stations. Late in the night of January 29, a Katusha rocket ripped through the roof of the Republican Palace and into PCO offices. It did not explode, but its impact killed two Americans working there.

For me, January 30—Election Day—began at six o'clock in the morning with multiple explosions that rattled the windows and sent me to the floor. I crawled into the living room and turned on CNN, which soon reported poll workers had failed to turn up at a polling location north of Baghdad. (It turned out CNN was in the wrong location.) As polling places opened, reports filtered in that the turnout was very light. It looked as though our worst fears might be realized.

At breakfast, everyone was glum. It was a three-day holiday for our Iraqi staff, with the exception of about a dozen people who had volunteered to stay and ensure all of our systems in the compound remained operational. I saw a few at breakfast and asked them if they would be able to vote. Their responses were indifferent. No one expressed any desire to vote, and several indicated their wives and relatives were too afraid to vote. Depressed, I drove to the palace. We were locked down, and all I could do was wait for reports from the military and our sources at the Electoral Commission. The only good news was the explosions seemed to have stopped. It was uncommonly quiet.

Throughout the morning I continued to receive reports from Jennifer Link. With a few exceptions in the Sunni Triangle, it seemed the polling stations were open across the country. Thousands of Electoral Commission employees, as well as some ten thousand domestic election monitors whom we had trained, were in place. The polling materials had been moved from secret warehouses in time for the polls to open. Turnout in the safer Shiite areas was heavy, as was turnout in the Kurdish north. Reports from the Sunni areas were spotty. In Baghdad, turnout was very light. Jennifer's reports matched what I heard from military officers who kept stopping in to trade information.

At about eleven o'clock, I started to receive calls on my cell phone from Iraqi employees who had talked to their relatives and to other employees outside the Green Zone. As the morning progressed, the Iraqi people saw that Coalition and Iraqi security forces had succeeded in clearing the streets and suppressing the insurgency. Coalition forces had set up standoff cordons away from polling places, with Iraqi forces providing security inside the cordons. As the citizens of Baghdad began to venture from their homes and talk to their few neighbors who had voted, they became increasingly emboldened. What began as a timid trickle became a flood of entire neighborhoods defying the insurgents and marching as phalanxes to polling places.

Pete Chiarelli, who was flying in a Black Hawk over the city, later told me it was the most amazing sight he had ever seen. Empty streets filled with citizens who were determined to vote for the first time in their lives in free elections. My phone rang almost nonstop with calls confirming that Baghdad residents were voting in large numbers. It looked as if we—we and the Iraqis—might pull this off.

By mid-afternoon, it was clear something truly extraordinary and historic was happening. We were euphoric, a completely foreign emotion regarding our experience in Iraq. At about two in the afternoon, I received a call from Fernando Cossich, who was at the compound. The Iraqi crew members who had volunteered to stay on duty had received calls from their families, urging them to vote. Fernando asked if there was any way we could arrange it. I called Jennifer, who sprang into action and arranged for them to vote at the single polling station inside the Green Zone. Fernando's deputy, Drew Parrell, put them all in a van and delivered them there.

Late in the afternoon, I returned to the compound. Drew had hastily arranged a barbecue for the Iraqi employees, who asked us to drop by. The indifference I had witnessed in the morning had turned to elation. They were dancing and holding their purple-inked fingers in the air. Several confided, with tears in their eyes, that this single act of voting was the most moving thing they had ever done or felt. When Jennifer arrived, she was mobbed. It was the high-water mark of my tour.

Ken Cox later told me that without that day, his tour would have been a failure. At a small dinner for the election team hosted by Ambassador Negroponte, Carlos Valenzuela said of all the elections with which he had been involved, this one had moved him like no other. He admitted, overcome with emotion, to shedding more than a few tears. We all felt that way.

We would learn later that 57 percent of the electorate had voted. The turnout among the Kurds and Shiites had been even stronger. The Sunnis had barely turned out, either out of fear of the insurgents or in adherence to their leaders' calls to boycott the elections. The main alliance of Shiite parties had won 48 percent of the vote; the Sunnis, barely 8 percent. The single-district system Bremer had agreed to before his departure eight months earlier had virtually assured the elections would result in a Shiite majority. Perhaps it was inevitable. Still, I remembered the conversation with the OGA operative six months earlier, when I had asked what just getting through the elections would get us. "A Shia government," he had replied.

"Then you will have a civil war," I had exclaimed.

17 WINDING DOWN

After the elections, we saw an immediate lull in the insurgents' attacks. Many pundits speculated the elections' success was a tipping point, and the Sunni insurgents had lost the initiative. Indeed, it soon became clear many Sunni leaders realized boycotting the elections had been a strategic error. My military friends hoped the lull meant the insurgents were demoralized, but they cautioned that the high tempo of pre-election attacks had undoubtedly diminished their capability. Perhaps the insurgents were just resting and rearming. Whatever, Baghdad and the rest of the country were comparatively quiet.

Condoleezza Rice had been sworn in as secretary of state on January 28. In early February, she dispatched an assessment team to Iraq, led by Ambassador Richard Jones. I had worked with Dick in Washington and served under him when he was ambassador to Lebanon. In the CPA, he had been the principal deputy to Bremer. Others on the assessment team included Maj. Gen. Raymond Odierno, Ambassador Robin Raphel, Dr. Philip Zelikow, Roman Martinez, and Jim Kunder. Robin had arrived in Iraq with Jay Garner and stayed on in the early days of the CPA as a senior adviser. Roman Martinez had been among Bremer's inner circle. Dr. Zelikow was an academic from the University of Virginia and would soon be named as counselor to Secretary Rice. Jim Kunder was my boss in Washington. Major General Odierno had been commander of the 4th Infantry Division in Tikrit when it captured Saddam Hussein.

None of us in Iraq were particularly enthusiastic about the assessment team's visit. Bill Taylor had already endured a second realignment of the supplemental in November and did not relish another. We had all been subjected to the eight-thousand-mile screwdriver when Secretary Rice was at the NSC. An assessment team's arrival a week after her swearing in did not bode well. It is axiomatic in government that an assessment team will make recommendations for change. This team was made up of highly qualified individuals, but we worried some of the former CPA members might carry a great deal of baggage. We had already been through painful adjustments and thought we were now moving together in the right direction. We did not want more changes for the sake of change and especially when they would lead to more broken promises to Iraqi ministers. Nevertheless, we swallowed hard and welcomed the team.

Dick Jones was keen on shifting more support to agriculture and the provincial governments. While I was an advocate of agriculture support and had successfully fought for $100 million to fully fund our efforts, I did not believe the ministry or we needed more supplemental funds. We had a massive local governance program, and I pointed out that Deputy Prime Minister Barham Salih had expressed his willingness to dispense $200 million to each of Iraq's eighteen governorates but only on a performance basis. We did not need to give U.S. supplemental funds to the provincial councils; instead, we needed to convince the new Iraqi government to give *its* funds to the councils and then use our governance program to ensure the funds were used wisely and transparently. The assessment team listened politely and then flew off to visit local officials in Kirkuk. Naturally, the local officials asked for funding—U.S. funding, that is.

The team also focused on another theme, generating short-term jobs, which we were already doing. The team asked why we could not initiate a works program on the magnitude of the Civilian Conservation Corps that President Franklin D. Roosevelt had championed in the United States in the 1930s. We pointed out that in Iraq camps of workers and exposed work sites would draw insurgent attacks and would, in any case, only have short-term impact. What Iraq needed was an improving economy that could provide and sustain long-term employment. In spite of the insurgency, the Iraqi economy was growing and generating employment, although not in all areas of

Iraq. We understood the importance of jobs, but a program of the magnitude the team suggested was beyond our means to deliver, especially given the security environment.

The assessment team members spent less than a week in Iraq and then flew back to Washington. Their recommendations would indeed lead to yet another realignment of the supplemental in March. Before they left, they asked me why we could not take $180 million from the supplemental and give $10 million to each of the provincial councils. I explained, again, that the Iraqi government could disperse its own funds, and I gave them three reasons why we should not use our appropriated funds. First, there was no practical, legal mechanism for us to do it. Next, the provincial councils would have great difficulty spending the funds, and we would not be able to account for them. Last, it would become an audit nightmare. Unfortunately, I knew I would hear more of this idea. And I did.

When I returned to Washington in March, one of the few meetings I had was with Meghan O'Sullivan. Previously a member of Bremer's inner circle, she was then responsible for Iraq and Afghanistan at the NSC. She asked how we could provide $180 million to the provincial councils. I reiterated the reasons we should not do it with appropriated funds and said that I could not imagine any mission director who would do so. Meghan gave me an inscrutable look and thanked me for my service.

Soon after the elections, Ambassador Negroponte departed for consultations in Washington. On February 17, I was watching the news when the president announced that he was nominating Ambassador Negroponte to be the new director of national intelligence. I was stunned. He had been in Iraq for only seven months. All of us thought he had done well. We had just had historic elections and were facing the critical stage of the new government's formation. It was not a propitious moment to change leadership at our most important diplomatic mission. At my next weekly meeting with Jim Jeffrey, I asked if he had known about the appointment in advance. He replied he had only been informed a few hours before the announcement. Later, Negroponte told me some discussions occurred before he left for Washington, but the nomination was not set until after he arrived.

I had great respect for Negroponte, and I believe that sentiment was universally shared in Baghdad. Some speculated Secretary Rice wanted her own man in the job he vacated and that the administration, with the U.S. elections behind it, wanted to shake things up, but this conjecture was muted. We were just sorry to lose him.

Although my one-year tour in Iraq would end on February 20, I had decided to stay up to a month longer. We had been working closely with Bill Taylor and his staff to adjust the electricity and water portfolios to accomplish as much as possible with the reduced resources now available in those sectors. Much to some people's surprise, I had agreed to cancel Bechtel's task order for the Mansuria gas plant and gas turbine generators—a $500 million project. It was a painful decision, given that it involved exploiting a gas field north of Baghdad and generating over 200 megawatts of new power. It was the largest project in our portfolio, and neither my staff nor Bechtel wanted to withdraw and hand it over to the ministries of oil and electricity. But Bill Taylor was trying to concentrate on electricity and water projects that could be completed in the least amount of time. I supported this effort, but it was still painful.

We were also going through Bechtel's other task orders, with Bechtel's and IRMO's full cooperation, and deciding where we could scale back our involvement. At the same time, we convinced them we should take on some new task orders, particularly in operations and maintenance training and equipment. For the past year, my engineers had been arguing that we were building systems the Iraqi ministries would not be able to operate and maintain, but it was not until after some of the first were delivered, and failed, that our arguments gained any traction.

Many adjustments were taking place, and I wanted to leave my successor with a reasonably clean slate and mandate. We were also receiving replacements for a significant portion of our senior staff, and I did not want to leave until the new people were in-country. My own replacement, Dawn Liberi, had only recently been selected, and it appeared she was not going to arrive until April or May. Bill Taylor and I argued to Washington that she needed to be in Iraq by March but to no avail. Jim Kunder, who had visited Iraq on several occasions—once for a full week—wanted me to extend my tour further, but he did not pressure me. My own view was that I had done enough. If Washington would not put a priority on getting my replacement to Iraq concurrent with my departure, so be it. I had been telling them for months that Deputy Director Chris Milligan, Infrastructure Director Bob Macleod, Program Director Teddy Bryan, and I all planned to leave on March 10. Chris and Bob had both been in Iraq for almost two years, and Teddy needed surgery. It was time for all of us to go.

Meanwhile, the V94 generator was still sitting in Jordan. Week after week at the SVTC, I endured the third degree from an increasingly exasperated and skeptical audience. The bridges had been shored, part of the route across the desert had been graded or repaired, and the elections were over. We continued to push the military to give us a date, but the move was postponed again and again. I dreaded my last SVTC, when I would have to say my farewells and tell them that the V94 was still sitting in Jordan. Fortunately, at my last SVTC, I was able to give an imminent date when the V94 would begin its journey to Iraq. It started a few days after I left and arrived a few weeks later at the site, without mishap or casualties.

During my last month in Iraq, Brig. Gen. Tom Bostick invited me to address the Society of American Military Engineers. I shared the dais with Gen. George Casey, Bostick, Bill Taylor, and Charlie Hess. The event was held in the Convention Center and attended by several hundred military officers and civilians, mostly from IRMO, PCO, and the Army Corps of Engineers. Many in the audience were distressed over the cuts to the infrastructure program, and they knew that USAID and "soft projects" had been the beneficiaries of those cuts. I was the last to speak.

I said even though USAID had $2.4 billion in infrastructure projects, I thought it had been a mistake to try to rebuild Iraq's infrastructure. We should have concentrated from the beginning on security, democratic governance, and economic policy reform and heavily emphasized smaller projects at the community level, much as we had belatedly done with the 1st Cav. We should have been more strategic in our selection of large infrastructure and concentrated on delivering electricity in Baghdad, the country's political center. The CPA's decision to distribute available electricity equally was very egalitarian, but it had resulted in an immediate 50 percent cut to every home in Baghdad. Saddam Hussein had kept the lights on in Baghdad while leaving the rest of the country in the dark for a good reason. We, too, should have kept the lights on in Baghdad. We should have focused on providing smaller cities with smaller and more easily provided generating units, thus avoiding the need for transmitting electricity over vulnerable transmission lines. We probably should not have worried about sewage treatment plants at all. They had been broken for decades. Bypassing them for a few more years would have made little difference. Most important, we should have followed the script we had used in other post-conflict countries: keep the lights on and water flowing, prevent health and food crises, and work rapidly to create—through good governance and legal reform—an enabling environment that would encourage both domestic and foreign investment in the infrastructure needed for a modern country.

Fully expecting to be booed from the room, I was surprised at the vigorous applause and thoughtful questions I received. Many approached me and thanked me for my candor. In my last days, a number of officers and civilians also stopped by the office to thank me. If nothing else, the reaction was a measure of how far we had come. Had I made those remarks in public during the CPA's reign, I would have been put on the first plane bound for home.

One of my last official acts was hosting a luncheon for Pete Chiarelli and members of his staff. The 1st Cav was rotating back to Fort Hood, Texas, and handing over responsibility for Baghdad to the 3rd Infantry Division, commanded by Maj. Gen. William G. Webster. The luncheon, held at our cafeteria, was a way to welcome the 3rd Infantry Division and to thank Pete, Ken Cox, and all of the 1st Cav. We also expressed our hope that our partnership for reconstruction would continue. We all thanked each other and traded mementos.

Pete Chiarelli and I had a few minutes after the luncheon to talk. He was leaving in a few days. Most of his men were already in Kuwait, and members of his staff had already left. Our year was over.

We both knew how hard we had tried and how many opportunities had been missed. Pete had aged visibly, and so had I. We had nothing profound to say. We just thanked each other. I regretted that I would not be able to attend the formal change of command. I just had too much to do. It was the last time I saw him.

18 GOING HOME

My last days in the Green Zone were relatively quiet. The lull in violence was short lived, but then the insurgents directed their suicide attacks against police recruits and Shiite gatherings. The winners of the elections haggled over the spoils of power, and the optimism that had seemed universal on January 30 was slipping away.

Increasingly, though I was proud of what USAID had accomplished on my watch in spite of all the obstacles, I felt we were losing. Chris Milligan and I talked about it. The irony was that our part of the operation had gone well, but the patient was still dying. I could not look at the whole reconstruction effort and believe USAID had given its best while the outcome remained in doubt.

None of us who were leaving on March 10 wanted going-away parties, but the Iraqi staff insisted. Chris and I decided we would host an awards ceremony, where we could present certificates of appreciation and the major awards that we had pushed through the Washington bureaucracy in the past months. We chipped in to pay for it, telling the Iraqi staff that it was "covered."

Chris and I thanked the mission staffers, and I said a few extemporaneous words about each recipient as I handed out the awards. The Iraqis presented us with mementos. We were both emotional but managed to hold it together. The party started in the cafeteria and soon moved outside, where an Iraqi caterer was preparing shish kabob and lamb chops. The Iraqis had arranged for a DJ, and the music was so loud we received complaints from the chancery. We kept turning it down, and the Iraqis kept turning it up. As the afternoon lengthened and the crowd thinned, I shared drinks with individuals and said good-bye. We had all been through so much together. I had already reached that point where I was there in body, but my spirit was moving away. It had happened thus at all of my postings, but the sense of being out of body was more intense this time.

My last country team meeting was on March 9. The day began with a terrific explosion, as a suicide bomber detonated his truck across the river. Ambassador Negroponte had returned and chaired the meeting. I had asked Chris, Teddy, and Bob Macleod to accompany me to this last meeting. When my turn to speak came, I thanked the ambassador, Jim Jeffrey, Bill Taylor, Charlie Hess, Steve Browning, and others for their support and for the opportunity to work with them. I then said that while I was the face of USAID they saw at each country team meeting, I wanted to acknowledge the people who stoked the coal and kept the engine running. I asked Chris, Teddy, and Bob to stand and said a few words about the contributions of each. They received the ambassador's thanks and a round of applause. Negroponte warmly thanked me for my service and my "candid counsel." As the meeting broke up, we chatted for a few minutes and said our good-byes. Afterward, Teddy and I went around to say good-bye to the many in the palace who had worked with us. We took one last look at the palace office, left it in Jadranka's capable hands, and drove back to the compound to pack.

Chris and I held our last meeting with our security team. Even though we were leaving, we had to make decisions about the trips into the Red Zone the next day. The job still had to be done, and a team would be going out as Chris and I were leaving. There had been an uptick in suicide car attacks, so we had to weigh the safety of sending people into the Red Zone. By this time, we both felt our supreme accomplishment was that none of our staff members had died, and we wanted to leave with no deaths on our watch. Chris, Fernando, DynCorp members, and I assessed the risk.

March 10, 2005, broke clear and cool. Through channels, Fernando and his crew had arranged Black Hawks to fly us to BIAP, where we would board an Air Serv flight for Jordan. It was a blessing we did not have to take the Rhino in the middle of the night. The cars and the full DynCorp detail to take us to the helipad were lined up next to the piazza. In spite of the early hour, a small crowd of our colleagues—expatriates and Iraqis—came by to see us off. Teddy was in tears, as were many of those we were leaving behind. I had hosted an impromptu gathering on my porch the previous evening and already said my good-byes. After a few hugs and handshakes on the piazza, I got in the car. Saying farewell was just too painful. I felt an overwhelming sense of loss and failure, and I was beyond more good-byes. The team going into the Red Zone was already assembling.

Fernando, Drew Parrell, and a few others accompanied us to LZ Washington. We had already turned in our body armor, and it felt odd to be traveling without it. Fernando and I smoked while we waited for the helicopters, which were late. Even though we had been through so much in Montenegro and Iraq—or perhaps because we had been through so much—we said little.

Finally, Fernando's radio crackled. The choppers were two minutes out. We watched them bank in and then turned our backs as the rotor wash swept dust and small stones over us. I gave Fernando an embrace and a thumbs-up and ran in a crouch for the second helicopter's door.

The Black Hawks were only on the ground for a few minutes. The door gunners signaled the pilots that we were strapped in, climbed aboard with their communication cables, and reloaded their machine guns. We lifted off and raced at low altitude across Baghdad. I strained to see below me the Baghdad that I had been so inadequate to help. In a few minutes, the dun houses and muddy streets of Baghdad gave way to the perfectly aligned trailers of Camp Victory. As the camp slipped under us, the pilots lined up on the military runway, landed, and deposited us on the tarmac. We were no longer important Coalition administrators. We were just four more people who were going home.

We dragged our bags across the gravel parking lot and searched for our ride. After waiting a few minutes, our expeditor and driver drove us around the end of the military runway to the civilian terminal. It did not look much different than when I arrived thirteen months earlier. Air Serv was delayed, and it looked for a while as if we were not going to get out that day and would have to spend the night at the airport. Finally, late in the afternoon, our flight arrived. We just managed to take off before the airport closed for the night. When the spiraling climb got us to 22,000 feet, the pilot leveled off and turned west. We all relaxed. We were safe.

All of us were booked in the same hotel in Amman and had planned to have dinner together. Most of us were leaving very early the next morning for flights to Europe and connections to the United States. The dinner was to be a wildly happy affair, giving us a chance to reminisce and savor the moment. We did have dinner and shared a couple of bottles of wine, but we were all so emotionally drained and physically exhausted we did little celebrating. Instead, dinner was a quiet and pensive affair, after which we stood outside the elevators, hugged each other, and said our good-byes.

I sat in business class on my final leg to Washington and watched an inane movie on the small screen swiveled in front of me. I do not remember if the plot involved a lost child or a lost dog, but I suddenly realized tears were running down my cheeks. I was on the verge of sobbing uncontrollably. Emotions I did not know were there just broke loose.

It was over.

EPILOGUE

We all went our separate ways. John Negroponte left Iraq in March, was sworn in as the director of national intelligence, and later became deputy secretary of state. Jim Jeffrey stayed for a few months until the new ambassador, Zalmay Khalilzad, arrived. Jim then went on to be the counselor to the secretary of state for Iraq. Bill Taylor returned home in July 2005. After a stint in the West Bank and Gaza, he was named ambassador to the Ukraine. Chris Milligan attended the National War College and earned a master's degree. Teddy Bryan did the same at the Army War College and became the country director for USAID in Tajikistan. Fernando Cossich married Gordana ("Goga") Popovic, a brilliant Bosnian who had worked for Teddy in the program office. Both are with USAID in Tbilisi, Georgia.

Bob Macleod returned to Washington and then worked the tsunami disaster in Indonesia. He moved next to Pakistan and helped earthquake victims. Jennifer Link finished her tour in Iraq and took an assignment in El Salvador. Kirk Day left OTI and started his own firm. David Wall is in Egypt, trying to reform its economy. Most of our Iraqi staff members left USAID after our departure. Some immigrated to the United States or Canada, at least one with the aid of Fernando Cossich. Two are dead, victims of sectarian murder. Charlie Hess works for a private company, as does Admiral David Nash. Ambassador L. Paul Bremer III wrote a book about his year in Iraq. Lt. Gen. Peter Chiarelli returned to Iraq in January 2006 as the Coalition ground force commander. Ken Cox joined him a few months later.

After Iraq, I took a vacation and decided to retire. My last few months, I worked as a senior adviser to the State Department's Office of the Coordinator for Reconstruction and Stabilization, a new organization tasked with responding to post-conflict, failed, and failing states. I retired on September 30, 2005. A few days later I visited Afghanistan as part of an interagency team that assessed the impact of provincial reconstruction teams, the joint military-civilian efforts designed to stabilize and reconstruct rural areas. In November, I went to work for a private company, where I focus on the Iraqs and Afghanistans of the future. I currently advise, lecture, write articles, participate in war games, and train soldiers deploying to Iraq. I try to give them the skills they need to keep them alive.

Stuart Bowen, the special inspector general in Iraq, has fairly and accurately documented what went wrong in Iraq. T. Christian Miller's *Blood Money* and Rajiv Chandrasekaran's *Imperial Life in the Emerald City: Inside Iraq's Green Zone* (Knopf, 2006) have documented not only what went wrong but also the excesses of imperial behavior that made it go wrong. Stuart Bowen's staff interviewed me multiple times, and he and I have often talked about what went wrong and what went right. David Nash, Bill Taylor, and I also gave interviews to T. Christian Miller. The *Foreign Service Journal* has published my views on civilian-military cooperation in war zones, I train brigades deploying to Iraq on counterinsurgency, and I have lectured at the Command and General Staff College, the Army War College, and Georgetown University on counterinsurgency, on conflict and post-conflict, and on how we must do better.

I believe we are slowly—oh so slowly—moving toward a better understanding of what we must do in the future. But we are not yet there. There is not much public enthusiasm left for policing the world. I do not believe the United States can or should be the world's policeman, but I do believe the United States is the only country with the moral imperative and capability to make a difference. We have only begun to understand our shortcomings, despite the lessons we have learned and earnest analyses by the State Department and the Defense Department. We still need to create the standing capacity to aid failing and failed states, even those at war. We have not yet done so, and now, as a private citizen, that is what I try to rectify.

Our experiences in Iraq and Afghanistan have painfully reminded us that we will not always have the luxury of fighting the precise kind of conventional, symmetrical war at which we are best. The military's experience in Vietnam was so searing and destructive that it buried the lessons of counterinsurgency. The military simply decided never again to engage in a conflict unless it could deploy overwhelming force and superior technology; however, the occupation of Iraq and the commitment to Afghanistan have forced the Pentagon to dust off its counterinsurgency lessons. Extraordinary officers have been instrumental in pushing the rewriting and updating of field manuals; and DOD Directive 3000.05 raised stability operations to the same level of importance as combat operations while directing greater interaction with civilian agencies, even during combat operations.

National Security Presidential Directive 44 established the principle that the Department of State, in cooperation with the military and appropriate civilian agencies, shall lead stabilization and reconstruction efforts abroad. The State Department Coordinator for Reconstruction and Stabilization (S/CRS) is supposed to lead this effort, but Congress has repeatedly refused to provide adequate funding for S/CRS to perform its mission. Without serious civilian efforts to establish the capability to respond quickly, the military is developing this capacity within its ranks. It has no choice but to do so. It will be a mistake and a lost opportunity, however, if the United States fails to develop a standing force of experienced civilians ready to respond anywhere in the world as rapidly as the military can.

Establishing such an organization is not difficult; it requires only national will and funding from Congress. An available field force of experienced, committed civilian practitioners is already contemplated and within reach. S/CRS has planned for civilian advance teams that would deploy both with the military and in circumstances where there is no military presence, but it has no funding to adequately implement the concept. Without a standing capacity, our civilian response will continue to be ad hoc and, too often, inadequate. The U.S. military cannot be expected to rely on a force that exists only on paper, and the country should not have to rely on the military to undertake what are essentially civilian functions. Unfortunately, counterinsurgency's emphasis on winning populations—not territory—does not clearly delineate where responsibility passes from the military to the civilian practitioner. A misstep in the combat phase can make stabilization efforts either daunting or impossible. Military and civilian practitioners must train together and learn the same doctrine if they are to deploy together as an effective force. They must deploy as a team, already known to each other, already integrated, already playing from the same book. Ironically, while prominent members of Congress, the Pentagon, State, and the military all understand this concept, funding for the civilian side of the equation is still not forthcoming.

What of Iraq? Though this book is not a tome about policy, I have sufficiently paid my dues in the Middle East and Iraq to venture an opinion.

The Ottoman Empire's three provinces of Kurdistan, Baghdad, and Basra, which were equivalent to the Kurdish north, the Sunni center, and the Shiite south, make up present-day Iraq. After World War I, the British and the French carved up the Ottoman Empire. Gertrude Bell and Winston Churchill created the nation of Iraq after a debilitating insurgency that inflicted more than twenty thousand casualties on British colonial troops. They installed as king a Hashemite from Mecca.

Few countries in the Middle East enjoy a true national identity. Most are riven by sectarian and ethnic differences, only coming together in national unity when threatened by a foreign power. (The Shia provided the fodder in the 1980–88 Iran-Iraq War—on both sides.) The Assad family, who brutally rule Syria, are Alawites, which make up 10 percent of a predominantly Sunni population. Lebanon is an accommodation of disparate Christian, Druze, Sunni, and Shiite sects. Its constitution attempts to ensure peace by sharing power among religious factions, but instead ensures the lowest common denominator in governance. An aging king and six thousand princes rule Saudi Arabia. The Gulf States are fairly homogenous, and most are trying to modernize, albeit with a guest workforce mainly from Lebanon, Egypt, and South and Southeast Asia. Jordan is reasonably stable, with a Hashemite monarchy, but it hosts a Palestinian population that outnumbers the Hashemite Bedouins. It has been the target of Al Qaeda and is threatened by its neighbors' insecurity.

Egypt is an autocracy, in spite of billions of dollars of U.S. assistance. Free elections would probably bring an Islamic government to power in this most populous country in the Middle East. Without Egypt, there can be no successful war against Israel. We count on that fact, and we tolerate and support Egypt's authoritarian government even with the sure knowledge that it is a hotbed of political frustration and potential violence. Our allies in the Middle East are now on the defensive. They will ultimately look to their own deportment—meaning they will do what they have to do to survive, regardless of what the United States perceives to be in its own interests.

Once we vanquished Saddam Hussein, the Shiites, and particularly Grand Ayatollah Ali al-Sistani, knew their time had come. Sistani used Bremer and the Coalition, and he played on our democratic principles. The Shiites had been brutally suppressed under Saddam Hussein, although in Iraq they outnumbered all other groups combined. Democratic elections, in a region where citizens vote their tribe and religion, would bring the Shiites to power. Thus, Sistani only had to play the Westerners' game and refuse to diverge from his playbook. All he had to do was demand that the Coalition, but mainly the Americans, stick to its own democratic principles and notions of fair play concerning the Shiite majority, which had been savaged, denied, and persecuted. Sistani stymied Bremer at every turn and refused to talk to "the occupier." He stirred Iraqi patriotism against the invaders, while using them to institute the very democratic reforms that would ensure Shiite control of Iraq. Sistani would not budge on his demands for the national election of an Iraqi government that would draft a constitution to be put to a national referendum.

I do not believe Sistani envisioned a clerical Iraq, beholden to Iran. He was a shrewd statesman in a sea of sharks. He knew national elections would result in an Iraq ruled by a Shiite majority. If that failed, his fallback—a Shiite state in the south of Iraq—was not a bad compromise. Thus, he kept his distance from the Americans and let them do his work for him. He was not being disingenuous, just pragmatic. He may have actually believed Shiites, Sunnis, Kurds, and Turkmen could come together and form a democracy. In the face of escalating Sunni attacks on Shiites, Sistani counseled against retaliation and warned against the dangers of sectarian violence that could spiral into civil war. After the February 2006 destruction of one of the Shiites' holiest shrines, the gold-domed Al-Askariya Mosque in Samarra, however, even Sistani gave up on the Sunnis. His silence signaled acquiescence to Shiite retaliation and the bloodbath of ethnic cleansing that has since reigned.

After the Coalition defeated Saddam's forces, the Sunnis were absolutely bereft. They had ruled over the Kurds and the Shiites, who outnumbered them, for a thousand years. Through Iraq's modern history and certainly under Saddam Hussein, the Sunnis had had the best jobs and the power. The conduct of the American occupation cemented their fears that their suzerainty was over. In their minds, Kurdish and Shiite domination was worse than death and had been imposed by a foreign power, by infidels. The American invasion had barely touched the Sunni heartland. The Sunnis had not faced American firepower—no Abrams tanks, no Bradley fighting vehicles, no overwhelming air power, no deadly infantry forces—but they did contend with American occupation. They soon discovered that Americans bled like everyone else, particularly when confronted with Muslims who were not afraid to die. We know the rest.

Kurdistan—a name we did not use in the CPA or later in the embassy—has existed in fact since 1991. The Northern No-Fly Zone ensured Kurdish autonomy. The Kurds made the most of it. Their political leaders, the Talabanis and the Barzanis, despite their traditional enmity, compromised and built a prosperous, nameless nation state that was already extant when we invaded Iraq. By 2006, it had its own flag, investment promotion regime, and two governments. Although the president of Iraq is a Kurd, as are other senior ministers in the Iraqi government, almost all Kurds want an independent Kurdish state. Kurds are purportedly the largest ethnic group in the world without their own country. Turkey, Syria, Iran, and Iraq all oppose a Kurdish state. Genuinely grateful to the Americans, Kurdish leaders pay dutiful lip service to the concept of Iraq as a unified state, because it is what the United States wants and because an independent Kurdistan cannot survive without U.S. protection. They know how to play the odds and bide their time. They have been doing it for centuries.

Our invasion of Iraq was a misguided mission of liberation, advised and promoted by well-meaning political appointees who believed American power knew no limits. They ignored history and the advice of talented career government employees who warned of such a mission's consequences. That Iraqis—Baathists, Shiites, Sunnis, Kurds, Turkmen, and Chaldean Christians—could always derail our plans for their future was ignored by our political leaders, who failed to realize that planning is just planning. I do not believe our leaders had a hidden agenda; instead, I think they were naive and consumed by arrogance and blind adherence to dogma. As a Vietnam veteran, I also feel great angst and anger that having had a small part in the loss of one war promulgated, prosecuted, and lost by arrogant leaders, I find myself at the twilight of my career involved in another war promulgated and prosecuted by people steeped in hubris and seemingly indifferent to all pleas for caution and introspection—and that I had voted for them.

Had we not allowed the security gap to open in Iraq and had we better planned its reconstruction, perhaps we could have bought enough time for a liberal democratic environment to develop in Iraq. But that outcome was always a tall order. If there was ever a window of opportunity for the Shiites, Sunnis, and Kurds to coexist in relative harmony, it rapidly closed, although I am not now convinced it was ever open. Too much history weighed against the Iraqis and us.

I no longer believe Iraq can survive as one nation. It is already divided, de facto, into the Shiite south and the Kurdish north. The Sunni center, which includes half of Baghdad, is in anarchy. The writ of the Iraqi government does not extend beyond the Green Zone. The Iraqi Sunnis will tell you that the Shiite south and the Kurdish north have all the oil. These regions do have most of what has been discovered but not all of it; most of Al Anbar, which is overwhelmingly Sunni and constitutes one-third of Iraq, has barely been explored. I do not believe the Kurds or the Shiites will share their oil wealth with the Sunnis, nor will they establish a fund modeled on the Alaska Permanent Fund. I do believe the Iraqis can eventually come to an accommodation that separates their territory into three nations, but it must be their idea and not ours.

The Kurds are already our allies. The Shiites are Arabs, not Iranians, and certainly not Persians; they share a common religion with Iranians, not a common destiny. We need to reach a reasonable accommodation with the Sunnis, and we cannot do that while we are fighting them. Theirs is a revenge culture whose roots lie in the great Arab conquests of the seventh century and the establishment of the caliphate. They will not give up, certainly not to infidels, and they will not consent to be ruled by Shiites and Kurds any more than the Kurds or Shiites will return to the past Sunni domination.

An autonomous Kurdish north is a reality. The Shiite south is moving rapidly toward autonomy, thought this will likely be cemented only after further factional bloodletting within the Shiite community. The center is messy. It is not all Sunni, particularly Baghdad. Partition would be difficult and probably violent, as it was in India in 1947, but it is doable. We have to admit to the facts on the ground.

We also have to admit that we have been bled in Iraq. The fear factor that held our enemies at bay is lost, not only in Iraq but also in the region and around the world. We have lost the goodwill of our allies. We need a political solution in Iraq, and we need bold thinking from our leaders and from the Iraqis. Staying the course is not a strategy, nor will the answer be found with the United Nations or our few remaining allies. It awaits an American president who can admit our country's failures but also convince the world that our values and our aspirations for the Iraqi people are viable and pure. It will also require, perhaps only after much more bloodshed, the understanding of Iraqi leaders that Iraq is not more than its disparate parts. It never was.

APPENDIX

A BRIEF HISTORY OF THE ECONOMIC GROWTH PROGRAM IN IRAQ

by David Wall

The United States Agency for International Development (USAID) began operations in Iraq in March 2003 with strategic programs in infrastructure, democracy, economic growth, health, and education. The economic growth program was comprised of two portfolios—economic governance, contracted to BearingPoint, and agricultural reconstruction and development, contracted to Development Alternatives, Inc. (DAI). While the DAI contract was awarded through a full and open competition, the BearingPoint contract was awarded under a limited competition waiver in support of a contingency operation.

The economic governance program commenced mobilization in March 2003, reporting to the Office of Reconstruction and Humanitarian Assistance (ORHA) through USAID. However, when ORHA was disbanded in May of that year and subsumed by the Coalition Provisional Authority (CPA), the new CPA administrator, Ambassador L. Paul Bremer, conducted a comprehensive review of all USAID programs and concluded that the economic governance program was not needed. In Bremer's opinion, economic policy reform work would be handled by the Department of the Treasury's Office of Technical Assistance and assisted by employees on loan from the Federal Reserve.

USAID held a series of meetings with Ambassador Bremer and his staff, outlining the costs associated with mobilizing such a contract and explaining the subsequent demobilization would result in additional costs to the American taxpayer. What's more, highlighting recent work in such theaters as Afghanistan, Kosovo, and Bosnia (to name but a few), USAID made a compelling argument that our vast experience in managing post-conflict economic transitions would be an added benefit to the CPA's efforts. Ambassador Bremer finally agreed, with the caveat that he would personally approve all activities carried out by BearingPoint. Accordingly, what had originally been agreed to in the scope of work was amended, and the program became a "job-order" contract.

Subsequently, CPA advisers would request assistance from USAID (in the form of BearingPoint advisers) by drafting a scope of work for discrete activities. USAID would then prepare an action memorandum for funds to be expended, identifying the number of advisers and level of effort, for Ambassador Bremer's signature. In total, the CPA tasked BearingPoint with thirty-eight activities, and by September 2004, thirty-two of those activities had been completed while the remaining six were canceled. This list of activities spanned every aspect of the CPA's mandate, from converting the Iraqi currency to developing a master plan for Iraq's electricity sector.

The budget story with respect to economic governance is an equally convoluted tale. The original contract was funded out of the Iraq Relief and Reconstruction Fund (IRRF I) emergency supplemental appropriations bill in 2003. The total contract value was $79.5 million, of which $78 million was obligated in early summer 2003. However, after revising the scope of work and ceding authority and control of the contract to the CPA, $35 million of funding was "de-obligated" from the contract in August 2003 to fill a funding gap in the infrastructure arena. This de-obligation was part of a "gentleman's agreement" between Ambassador Bremer and then–mission director Lew Lucke, who agreed the monies would be repaid to USAID when the second supplemental appropriations bill (IRRF II) became available in the spring of 2004. However, when the second supplemental appropriations bill was passed by Congress and the $18.4 billion IRRF II became available, much to USAID's surprise it had no line item for those activities being carried out under the economic governance scope of work. USAID appealed to the CPA's representative from the Office of Management and Budget (OMB), Rodney Bent, and was told that the monies "borrowed" from the BearingPoint contract were buried under two line items in the IRRF II, business skills training and vocational training.

At that time, the procedures for programming IRRF II funds were under development. The CPA's preliminary consensus was USAID should seek the concurrence of the CPA advisers who were in charge of overseeing those component activities. Maj. Martha L. Boyd, the CPA's adviser to the Ministry of Labor and Social Affairs (MOLSA), was more than accommodating in facilitating funds from the vocational training line item, which fell under MOLSA's purview. She understood the issue, was pleased with the explanation of events, and, when she was able to confirm the agreement between Bremer and Lucke, effected the transfer in a timely fashion.

Conversely, Michael P. Fleischer, deputy director of the CPA Office of Private Sector Development and the brother of Ari Fleischer, then–White House spokesman, was less accommodating. In Fleischer's view, additional funds deposited into a line item that he oversaw was a windfall for his office. He was not interested in any "gentleman's agreement" that had been struck and was even less interested in hearing anything that had to do with the BearingPoint contract. Only after repeated requests by the new USAID mission director, Spike Stephenson, and the eventual intercession of Rodney Bent's successor, George Wolfe, did Fleischer reluctantly agree to the transfer. Notably, because of Fleischer's reluctance to comply with the agreement, BearingPoint had begun demobilization, and scarce funds that could have been applied to the reconstruction of Iraq were diverted to cover these demobilization costs.

The agriculture program also began mobilization in March 2003. Working closely with ORHA, DAI mobilized some fifty advisers to spread across the country and to begin working closely with the Ministry of Agriculture in support of this program. However, like the economic governance program, when ORHA was disbanded and the CPA established, Ambassador Bremer conducted a review and concluded agriculture—the largest employment sector in Iraq, be it agriculture or agribusiness related—was not one of the CPA's priorities. Accordingly, of the $35 million obligated to the program for mobilization and start-up, Ambassador Bremer ordered the deobligation of $30 million for "other priorities" and left only $5 million for agriculture. USAID made several appeals to Bremer, but they fell on deaf ears. Without other funding sources available and with little support from the CPA, USAID ordered the contract's near complete demobilization. DAI sent the bulk of its advisers home by September 2003.

At this time, we started to think creatively and began to focus on what activities could be achieved with the limited resources available. The first priority identified was transforming Iraq's Stalinist approach to agriculture and getting the state out of the way. DAI was tasked with developing a "transition plan" for the Ministry of Agriculture. Lifting subsidies, removing price controls, and encouraging private sector investment were all part of the plan. The second area of intervention was developing "pilot programs," since without the full level of funding a comprehensive agricultural development program would be impossible. However, discrete pilot programs would be established as a way of demonstrating to the Iraqis what could be done. Seed-cleaning techniques, crop improvement technology, and soil salinity were just a few of the programs that DAI was able to deploy in support of the ministry's efforts.

Over time, as the U.S. military's civil affairs units began to disperse around Iraq, DAI began to leverage its pilot programs with the efforts of the civil affairs units. Seed-cleaning machinery, sheep-dipping tanks, distribution of vaccines, and veterinary training were all closely coordinated between the program and the U.S. military. Further, as the CPA took steps to prevent the collapse of Iraq's fragile Public (food) Distribution System (PDS), the program worked closely with the military to assist the Iraqi Grain Board, Ministry of Agriculture, and the Ministry of Trade to ensure wheat, rice, and foodstuffs were arriving in the country in a timely fashion. (It is noteworthy that a separate DAI contract was awarded for restoring Iraq's marshlands; however, this activity was funded by and run out of the Asia Near East Bureau (ANE) in Washington. When the contract vehicle for the marshlands expired, USAID rolled those activities under the existing agriculture program in September 2005.)

In the spring of 2004, pressure was mounting in Congress over the issuance of "sole source," or limited competition, contracts in the initial phase of Iraq's reconstruction. The original BearingPoint contract had been awarded under limited competition with a base period of one year and two option years that could be exercised. Mission Director Spike Stephenson instructed the Economic Growth (EG) Office that the option years would not be exercised and preparations should be made for follow-on activity. This task was to prove monumental. The instructions were given to the economic governance team in March 2004; the existing BearingPoint contract was scheduled to conclude in September of that year. The EG team (with the help of the Office of Iraq Reconstruction [OIR] Task Force and others in Washington) had to develop a completely new scope of work and to conduct a full and open competition in less than six months to avoid any disruptions in assistance to the Iraqis.

The original scope of work was drafted in less than two weeks with a number of subsequent revisions. However, when the time came to complete the government cost estimate for the scope of work, the procurement appeared to run more than $500 million dollars. While not a remarkable sum in the context of Iraq's reconstruction effort, it would have represented the largest economic development program ever conceived by USAID and would certainly represent a significant challenge for even the most experienced USAID implementing partners. The decision was quickly made to split the procurement between the "policy" type reforms and those activities that were largely "private sector-led." Accordingly, the Economic Governance II Project and the Private Sector Growth and Employment Generation (later to be named IZDIHAR) programs were born.

Again, Mission Director Stephenson instructed Washington to fast-track this procurement. However, one minor issue prevented it from happening: there was no funding for these programs. The agriculture program was on life support, squeaking by with $5 million in funding and later receiving incremental funding of $4 million from the infrastructure portfolio for support of irrigation techniques (USAID could not be faulted for creative thinking), and the BearingPoint contract was burning through its funding apace, all the while supporting the CPA in myriad activities. In sum, USAID was going to have to look for funding if it was to award these contracts.

At that time, the only funding USAID's economic governance portfolio had from the IRRF II was dedicated to a vocational training program that USAID was asked to implement on the CPA's behalf. Designed by CPA advisers working in MOLSA, the CPA viewed the program as falling within USAID's field of expertise. USAID made several attempts to refine the scope of work based on numerous lessons learned in vocational education (Voc-Ed) efforts in similar countries; however, the CPA refused to alter the program. It is worth noting the CPA advisers who rebuffed USAID's efforts were two civil affairs officers who had little experience in designing and developing vocational training programs. Both reservists, one was the owner of a construction company and the other a fireman.

At this point, Mission Director Stephenson instructed the EG team to employ more of that creative thinking that had become so necessary in Iraq. The vocational training program had approximately $80 million allocated from the IRRF II that was readily available. Spike and his team pushed a proposal to "borrow" $40 million from that $80 million and allocate it evenly between economic governance and private sector development so these procurements could proceed. Their logic was that when the U.S. embassy succeeded the CPA in June 2004, USAID would appeal to the incoming ambassador for a realignment of IRRF II funds, and these two contracts would receive their appropriate allocations. With the new allocations, USAID would pay back the funds borrowed from the vocational training program and carry the programs forward for the next fiscal year. However, given the unique nature of this proposal and that USAID was talking about an IRRF II reallocation (the IRRF II funds had only just become available, and procedures had not even been established), this proposal would require not only the approval of the CPA senior advisers but of Paul Bremer himself.

Once again, USAID reached out to Major Boyd of MOLSA, who was in her own right a bit concerned with this rather high-risk proposal. She raised the following concerns: When will the money be returned to the Voc-Ed contractor? What is the method of returning the money? Is it legal to do what we're proposing here and, if not, how can we ensure that the funds will definitely be returned for use in the MOLSA contract? She asked all legitimate questions for which, in some cases, we did not have answers (never mind we had no guarantee we could repay the money). Spike and his team were taking a large gamble that they would be able to convince the incoming ambassador (now known to be John Negroponte) to reallocate funds to USAID. One certainly could not fault Major Boyd for her line of questions or her concern; she had a job to do and a general to report to. Nevertheless, after an exhaustive round of consultation (which again, understand, was holding up the procurement while time slowly ticked away), she agreed. Spike Stephenson submitted the authorizing action memorandum to Ambassador Bremer, who signed it on June 27. The following day, Bremer left Iraq, and the CPA ceased to exist.

With the funding in hand, USAID aggressively moved to the procurements. Once again Spike called in a few chips with Washington and requested the assignment of two contract officers to be dedicated full time to getting these procurements done. Accordingly, John Lord and John Griffin were called to Washington to assist with this task. With the publication of the pre-solicitation notices in May, the requests for proposals hit the street on June 30, and both contracts were awarded by September 30, with $20 million obligated to Economic Governance (BearingPoint) for mobilization and $20 million to IZDIHAR (a consortium of the Louis Berger Group and The Services Group). To say mountains were moved to achieve this feat would do a disservice to the individuals who made it happen. It was one of the seminal successes of USAID's and the U.S. government's efforts in supporting Iraq's transition to a free-market economy.

With the success of the contract awards in hand, the next step in the process was securing additional funding to ensure these two programs were not stillborn (to say nothing of the agriculture program's impending demise). It would be one thing to mobilize these contracts and deploy a group of advisers, but by now fourteen months in Iraq had taught USAID that $20 million was not a great deal of money when one factored in the scope, scale, complexity, and, of course, security implications of what needed to be done. Again, timing was to play a critical role.

In July 2004, USAID made a presentation to Ambassador Negroponte, outlining the USAID portfolio and highlighting key issues (including the funding picture). Negroponte clearly saw that the original IRRF II allocation process had been less than transparent and that decisions regarding projects and budgeting had not included all the key stakeholders in Iraq (most notably USAID). More to the point, of the $18.4 billion allocated to Iraq as part of the IRRF II, less than 1 percent had anything to do with economic assistance or agriculture.

Ambassador Negroponte quickly called for a "strategic review" of the IRRF II so that all stakeholders could be given the opportunity to present their case. George Folsom and a team of OMB examiners arrived in Baghdad and began an exhaustive review of the entire U.S. reconstruction effort in July 2004. This more than two-week-long "puts and takes" exercise with numerous presentations provided by USAID technical staff and senior management culminated in the arrival of Gordon West, assistant administrator for ANE, for the final round of meetings with the Iraq country team. The sum effect of this effort was the reprogramming of $300 million in IRRF II funds to be split evenly among the economic growth contracts, with $100 million for economic governance, $100 million for IZDIHAR, and $100 million for agriculture. Once again, this achievement cannot be overstated. A great many individuals on the Iraq country team—both military and in the newly formed Iraq Reconstruction Management Office (IRMO)—all vied for funding to support their programs. The combined success of USAID in presenting its case to support this funding reallocation is a testament to the hard work of those individuals involved. While the funds would not ultimately become available until December 2004, USAID made good on its promise to Major Boyd and quickly took steps to reallocate the $40 million borrowed from the vocational training program. Most important, our rejuvenated programs renewed operations in earnest.

In the spring of 2004, USAID/Iraq had been asked to assist the CPA in designing and developing a business skills training program.

USAID enlisted the expertise of USAID offices in Washington and the Volunteers for Economic Growth Alliance (VEGA), a consortium of USAID nongovernmental organizations (NGOs) and contractors that provides technical expertise in private, public, and NGO sector development. Again, working with the CPA's Office of Private Sector Development, USAID developed a $5 million grant program that sought to work with the local Iraqi business centers (established under the CPA) and to assist Iraqi entrepreneurs in developing the necessary business skills to operate in a free-market economy. While some members of the economic growth team expressed their concern about mobilizing volunteers to a place like Iraq (in the spring of 2004 the first Sadrist uprising began), Washington insisted a similar program had been successfully implemented in Kosovo and would be able to operate in Iraq. With the 1st Cavalry Division's assistance, attempts were made to operate in Baghdad, but as the security situation continued to deteriorate, VEGA was relegated to operations in the Kurdish north. It eventually closed down its Iraq-based operations in 2005.

Finally, the aforementioned vocational training program represents the last of the contract vehicles under the supervision of USAID's economic growth portfolio. As stated, we had serious reservations with respect to this program's design. Nevertheless, agreement was finally reached with the CPA, and in March of 2004 USAID proceeded with procurement. After full and open competition, one of the competing firms protested the eventual award. The contracting officer issued a conditional notice to proceed, but poor management and equally poor staffing plagued the program. When USAID finally secured a staffing change (the chief of party was replaced), the Iraq Reconstruction Management Office requested a modification to the scope of work so the program could support an operations and maintenance module and augment the ongoing rehabilitation work being carried out on Iraq's infrastructure (most notably, the electricity and water and sewage sectors). Regrettably, USAID's contracting office felt such a modification to the scope of work would validate the protest of the procurement, and, in the early fall of 2005, the program was terminated for convenience. The remaining funds were transferred to the Iraq Reconstruction Management Office for an operations and maintenance program.

INDEX

ABOUT THE AUTHOR

James Stephenson received a bachelor's degree in English literature from the University of South Carolina in 1968, served four years as a U.S. Army officer (including a combat tour in Vietnam), and then received a juris doctor degree in 1975, also from South Carolina. After a brief stint practicing law, he joined the United States Agency for International Development (USAID) as a Foreign Service officer and subsequently served in Egypt, Barbados, Grenada, El Salvador, and Washington. In 1997 he was sworn in as USAID mission director to Lebanon, followed in 2001 by the same honor in the Federal Republic of Yugoslavia. In 2004 he was made USAID mission director to Iraq, where he served for thirteen months. Now retired from the Foreign Service, he writes, lectures, and trains military and civilian personnel in counterinsurgency. The father of two sons, he resides in Virginia with his wife.